Baden-Powell

A FAMILY ALBUM

Baden-Powell

A FAMILY ALBUM

Heather Baden-Powell

with a foreword by
LORD BADEN-POWELL,
3rd Baron Baden-Powell of Gilwell,
nephew of the author

ALAN SUTTON · Gloucester
HIPPOCRENE BOOKS, INC. · New York

First published in Great Britain 1986
Alan Sutton Publishing Limited
Brunswick Road · Gloucester

Reprinted 1990

British Library Cataloguing in Publication Data

Baden-Powell, Heather
Baden-Powell : a family album
1. Scouts and scouting—Great Britain—
Biography   2. Boy scouts
I. Title
369.43′092′4   HS3316.G7

ISBN 0–86299–273–7

First published in the U.S.A. 1986
Hippocrene Books, Inc.
171 Madison Avenue · New York · NY 10016

ISBN 0–87052–315–5

Typesetting and origination by
Alan Sutton Publishing Limited
Printed in Great Britain

To my son Michael

IN PROUD AND LOVING MEMORY OF
MICHAEL ROBERT HALL KING
BORN 26 SEPTEMBER 1942

MISSING ASSUMED DROWNED IN THE
DISASTER OF THE GREEK CAR FERRY
SS HERAKLION IN THE AEGEAN ON THE
NIGHT OF 7/8 DECEMBER 1966

This tablet is in the church of St Peter Ad Vincula,
South Newington, Oxfordshire.

In 1940 the author married Pilot Officer John King, RAFVR, and in 1942 produced her first son, Michael. Their second son, Timothy, was born in 1946. After the war her husband was given a permanent commission in the Royal Air Force and apart from home service they served in Greece, 1947–50, and Norway, 1964–66. After retirement in 1967 they farmed in Oxfordshire and bred thoroughbred horses until 1983, when they retired to Little Compton on the Oxfordshire, Gloucestershire and Warwickshire borders. The book is dedicated to their elder son who was drowned in the Mediterranean shortly after passing his final Architects' exams.

Foreword

Lord Baden-Powell, 3rd Baron Baden-Powell of Gilwell

When I was very young and at kindergarten I vividly remember one specific day when the whole school was called into the main assembly hall to see a film. This was a day that my wife also remembers for she was also there. The film was about the life of the Chief Scout of the World whose death had been announced that day, but as far as I was concerned the man in the film was my beloved grandfather with whom I had spent very happy times not so long previously. He was the first 'adult' to impinge upon my conscience, other than my parents and nannies, but then, to a little boy they were not adults.

To this day I remember that dreadful moment because it was the first time that someone who I loved had 'gone home' – a very Scout saying – and I cried and cried. The reason why I cried was because 'B-P' was the first *real* friend that I had ever had; I remembered how he had given all his time and energies to me when we were together; there was total, mutual trust such as I had never experienced with anyone else.

Of course what I had experienced with him was common to all the thousands of young people who had come into contact with him throughout his life; that innate ability to communicate which had such a startling effect and allowed the rapid spread of two world movements for the young.

To three children and three nieces he was just plain 'Dad', and in many ways a very different character. This book gives an insight of how B-P and his devoted wife appeared through the eyes of one of those children. Like all families there were dramas both good and bad, but, through these pages one can glimpse the sight of two great world figures, how they behaved in private, their thoughts and their attitudes to the adulation that they received, but most of all their innate sense of duty to the young. What does come over to great effect is that the charismatic 'hero of Mafeking' was, in fact, a very private and humble man not quite at ease with the mantle of world hero that had been thrust upon him. He had a slightly wicked sense of humour, inherited by his daughter in no small measure.

To be a child of one famous parent can be very

hard, but to be the child of *two* famous parents must be almost insurmountable at times. To us, in this spread and often fractured family, Heather King is the Queen. To those who know the family well she is a warm mirror of her famous parents, happy, generous, humble, thoughtful and kind – one can seldom travel far without someone coming up and saying 'What relation are you to my friend Heather?', or more usually, 'I was at school with Heather'. All I can add to that is that it must have been a *mighty* large school.

The Album Pages

On album pages R.B-P. and H.B-P. indicate the work of Robert Baden-Powell and Heather respectively.

CHAPTER ONE

1915-20

'In the Beginning was God' was what it said in my Bible. But as far as my memory carried me back, the Beginning was 'Bear'.

My father had just rescued me, aged three, from a huge 'German' who had come to the door of the old farmhouse in which we were living, Little Mynthurst in Surrey. A great bear-like man, dressed in furry flying suit, helmet and leather boots, occupied the whole of the doorway. I was terrified, being immediately convinced that he was 'the enemy from the War' – whatever that meant – and that he had come to kill us all.

All fear was banished when my father came and gathered me up in his arms and greeted the 'German'. He was none other than Ernest Court, who had been chauffeur to my parents since they had first owned a motor-car. There he stood, the Great War ended at last, straight back from the Royal Air Force (as it had recently become), still in his flying clothes, all furry. 'He's a bear' I declared defiantly, and 'Bear' he became to us all as he threaded his way back into the Baden-Powells' family life.

Olave Soames and Robert Baden-Powell had been married quietly on 30th October 1912. There were probably a few raised eyebrows in the family pew, with a bridegroom of 54 years, the bride but 22! Outside the church was the inevitable guard of honour of Scouts gathered to see them drive away in the new Standard car, given to them as a wedding present, to a house they had rented in Sussex, at Ewhurst Place. It must have been while living there that the car was first registered, as it had the Sussex registration letters of those ever-recurring initials – 'BP'.

It was at Ewhurst that Peter, Betty and I all duly came into this world. None of us could ever remember anything about the house except that we were always told what a lovely view it had across the Rother valley to the old ruined walls and moat of Bodiam Castle. When brother Peter was joined, a year and a half after his birth, by a little sister, there had been no hesitation in finding a name for her. Many years before, when staying with friends at Kiftsgate on the edge of the Cotswolds, my father – always a lover of little

children – had been enchanted by a plain little girl called Heather, and he mused to himself that, one day, should he ever have a plain little daughter of his own, he would call her Heather. So he did, and that is how I came to be named.

At about the same time as sister Betty was born, nearly two years later, came the sad news from France that the owner of Ewhurst had been killed in action and the house was now up for sale. As my parents could not afford to buy it (nor did they like it well enough to want to live there permanently) they uprooted from Sussex and moved to another rented house, this time in Surrey, with an easier train service to London.

Little Mynthurst was an old timbered farmhouse, black and white and beamy with creaking oak doors and wooden latches. Little Mynthurst had its charms but there were disadvantages too. The worst of its shortcomings were its ancient beams, low and exposed and the lintels over every doorway waiting to deliver a knock-out blow. My father, to avoid constant swearing, took to wearing his old fishing hat in the house – a green one with spare fishing flies kept in the ribbon-band.

The sloping nursery floor was the main fascination in our lives and by crawling down into one corner and pulling back the mat covering the bare boards, we children could peep down onto the heads of the people chatting in the drawing-room below, and could see that curious Burmese lamp on its stand of blue and white china elephants.

It was from here that my parents set forth on their quest for a permanent home; a home in which they could not only bring up three growing children, but could also tackle all the problems and help foster the growth of the rapidly expanding Boy Scout and Girl Guide (as they were then termed) Movements.

It was on bicycles that they sallied forth on their house-hunting expeditions, a petrol shortage being ever the problem as the war dragged on into its fourth year. As they bicycled on their way from Surrey into Hampshire they had on their house-agent's list of properties a place called 'Crocks' in Bentley. 'Quite – but only quite – nice' they thought. It was not as 'desirable' as the blurb made it out to be, 'secluded by a high brick wall', for it completely failed to state that it was situated right on the edge of a busy main road.

Despondently they were about to pedal on their way when they saw an open driveway and could not resist turning in to explore. They pushed on past the Lodge and up a long hill, stopping on the way to picnic on the grass verge. At the top of the hill they came to a gate, behind which stood a house nestling in an open space of lawn, sheltered to the west by a wood, with the drive taking a long left-hand sweep up to the door – the very house they had dreamed about and were looking for – long and low and mellow. There was only one thing to be done; they must go and knock on the door and see if it could be for sale.

They found Mrs Trimmer, a widow living alone with an airedale dog, Jack. Without even wanting to look over it, they promptly asked, 'Would you ever think of selling this house?'

She was somewhat taken aback but after due deliberation Mrs Trimmer decided that, yes, perhaps she would sell the house – and Jack the dog would go with it. She could find herself a smaller house in Surrey. In the event she found herself one so adjacent to Little Mynthurst that the removal van that brought our furniture was able, on its return journey, to take hers away.

The house was not very old, in fact it could have been classified as modern, though the red brick was nicely mellowed and the timber-work weathered. It had been built by Mr Trimmer – a partner in Payne's Toy Shop in Holborn – in the early part of the century, and he and his wife had lived here until his death in 1910. After a few years of solitude, Mrs Trimmer had begun to think of selling the place and when my parents came along so fortuitously on their bicycles, that hastened her decision.

The original name given to the house was taken from the adjoining copse called 'Black-acre'. This name did not appeal at all to the BPs and as it was on the day of the Armistice that they had found it (combined with my mother's aptitude for finding appropriate names for everything) they decided to call it Pax Hill.

So they packed us all up from Little Mynthurst – dogs, children, nurses, pigeons and doves – and the move took place in the winter snow of 1919. The donkey and cart were left to follow in their own time, in slow stages 'on the hoof', conducted by a young apprentice enlisted for the occasion from the local garage. Tiny tots though we must have been at the time, we could just remember the journey to Pax, with our best friend 'Bear' at the wheel of the Standard car, BP 717.

Little could we foresee as we tumbled out on to the driveway and ran back excitedly to watch the men digging out the removal van which had stuck in the snow, that we had arrived at a house which was to become known to people throughout the world. Many are the houses with a far longer history than Pax but it would be difficult to find one that made its name in so short a span of time. During the next twenty years, as the theme of Scouting and Guiding rapidly spread across the world, expressing the belief in training youngsters to be self-sufficient and to make use of the outdoor life, the inspiration and encouragement was directed from this one well-head, this spring, at Pax Hill in the heart of the Hampshire countryside.

CHAPTER TWO

1920-25

Pax Hill is the backdrop most vivid in all our childhood memories. It radiated happiness – with a few bumps and bruises – and it was our home for exactly twenty years, from the date of purchase in 1918 to my father's final journey to Kenya in the autumn of 1938.

A menagerie of animals gradually accumulated, as did household staff, led by Bear. Bear's sister Annie, who had been with the Soames family before my mother married, came to Pax ostensibly as the housemaid, but sometimes she was the cook and was even known to masquerade as parlourmaid. They had a sister who could cook, so it wasn't long before Mabel was installed with us too, to be followed by Lily, the parlourmaid, and Ethel, the housemaid, all arriving from Stoke Canon, the village in Devon from which this family unfailingly came. They came and then they all seemed to be snapped up in matrimony. 'As cooks go she was good – and as cooks go, she went.'

Annie's turn came eventually when Scofield came on to her horizon. Scofield's only claim to fame, as he told everybody, giggling as he said so, was that he had 'passed through' Sandhurst – but only on his coal lorry. Annie, however, was not for leaving Pax for a coal wagon, so it was duly arranged that we should employ Scofield as a gardener and he and Annie lived happily ever after in the Lodge at the foot of the drive up to Pax.

It was funny how frequently Bear came up to the nursery these days, to see how we children were getting on. We were getting on very well – now that we had our dear new Nursie. We had previously had one or two nurses to whom we had not taken kindly at all and one despatched herself because we'd decided to try screaming and screaming and SCREAMING until we gave her a headache – which, when reprimanded later, we were told we had done.

We hadn't cared for Nurse Winifred, or 'Win-niwed', either; she forbade us to mix water with the sand in our happy sand-house at the end of the pergola, because we made ourselves and our clothes in such a mess. Stalking games (obviously inherent in our blood and probably encouraged by

my father) led us round behind the flower border from where, undetected by nurse, we could get down into the ditch behind the coal shed, and creep along behind the garage to the rubbish heap. Here we would salvage a rusty old tin each, come back via the rain-butt at the corner of the wood-shed to gather up some water and then crawl carefully back to the sand-pit and triumphantly tip it in. When Winniwed called us in at bed-time, we quickly dispersed from the sand-house to our hiding positions in the bushes and tall pampas grass beyond. Belligerent little beasts we then were, defying discipline as well as poor Nurse Winniwed.

But now all was different, we had Nursie! All was different for Bear too, and it was not long before a lovely nursery romance was passing blissfully over our innocent little heads. When it was announced that Bear and Nursie were to be married, my father brought out his architect's drawing-board and designed a 'Den' for them. An opening was made in the hedge round the pad-dock and the 'Bear's Den' was built – half-timbered like Pax – on the opposite side of the drive from the spot where my parents had had their original house-hunting picnic. A Spanish chestnut tree stands nearby and the picnic place was now marked with a ring of logs forming a camp-fire circle where Scouts could come and camp on the wide verges of the drive and make their fires.

Not only had Bear and Nursie been set up with a home of their own but B-P had persuaded Major and Mrs Wade to migrate from Chelsea and helped them to find Ash Cottage in Bentley. Eileen Wade was my father's private secretary and has been the backbone of the B-P family for many years longer than her book *Twenty-seven Years with Baden-Powell* would lead one to suppose.

She first became involved when, as Miss Nu-gent, she wished, in the innocence of youth, to venture from her family home in Yorkshire to see what London had to offer a newly-qualified secretary or shorthand-typist. The hand of fate guided her through the doors of the Boy Scout office and she never really escaped again. Through the vicissitudes of two World Wars she remained as the nucleus of the Headquarters Staff. B-P had already spotted her ability and her personality and when she thought, at the end of hostilities in 1918, to hand over to the men returning from their military duties, he persuaded her not to leave.

Fate then cleverly played its part again; it brought a certain Major Wade home from Saloni-ka and B-P had soon delegated to him the task at the Scouts Headquarters of organizing the first World Jamboree ever to be held – staged at Olympia in 1920. All the correspondence, notes, ideas and papers that B-P wrote in preparation for this great event were handed to Miss Nugent who then handed them on to Major Wade. Miss Nu-gent and Major Wade were thus unremittingly flung together, whether they liked it or not. Luckily they liked it; they loved it, and as soon as the work of the Jamboree was safely over, they were married and went to live in Chelsea.

But a private secretary living in Chelsea was not the most convenient arrangement for my father and so it was generally agreed that the Wades should become citizens of Bentley too. Their new home, in winter time when trees were bare, was just within sight of Pax Hill.

With a well-established staff at Pax and the Wades close at hand, our parents were confidently able to leave us small people while they responded to requests from many parts of the country, as well as from overseas, to go and visit the troops and companies of Scouts and Guides and help to promote the Movement wherever it was most urgently necessary to keep it running on the right lines.

In 1919 they went off to America, where they were hailed by the rank-levelling press as 'Mr Powell and his daughter', and fulfilled a most hectic programme of meetings, lectures, civic receptions and conventions. My mother was thrown in at the deep end and quickly acquired the ability to make a speech. Not being in the least bit self-conscious, she was able to address audiences great or small; she trained herself from the start, spoke utterly spontaneously and never used notes. Rather, she said, did she prefer to adopt the attitude that she would give a talk and not make a speech.

The following year an urgent request came from India, where Scouting had been enthusiastically started but had split into six different groups; it was essential that B-P should come and draw them all together. One of these groups was led by the notable Englishwoman and disciple of Gandhi, Mrs Annie Besant. When agreement had finally been reached to blend the British and the Indian Scouts into one Association, it was duly recorded that 'We who had sat down to the table as a meeting of representative heads rose at the end of it a united band of Brother Scouts' – a great tribute to the achievement of this visit.

The only time my father ever forgot the words of the Scout Promise – devised by himself – was when Mrs Besant, 'picturesque in her native costume', stepped out to take the promise from him on behalf of all the leaders there. He lost himself and had to be prompted!

Whilst they were travelling and in spite of the immense pressure of the work involved, my parents managed to send letters home to us. Mother always wrote on her typewriter – her handwriting, she said, was too large and too slow. My father wrote in capital letters for the benefit of us little children and always embellished the pages with sketches, maps or drawings, and even a little verse.

Before their next voyage abroad and with Nursie's departure with Bear to 'The Den' (where they duly raised two little girl cubs) my brother Peter became a schoolboy in grey flannel suit and red cap and tie. He had a happy time at a school in Pyrford with his friend Ole Pooley, not so much in the class-room as in fishing for pigs over the school boundary wall, with improvised rod and line of sticks and string and with acorns for bait.

We two girls, joined by a couple of Davidson

cousins, inherited by my mother after her sister Auriol's death, now had a governess. She was a 'nursery governess' called Gam and as there now seemed such a crowd of us in the house, my father drew out his architect's board again. Already a servants' wing had been added to the east side of Pax and now B-P designed a fine west wing, built out into a corner of the rose garden, its herringbone brick blending in with the main part of the house.

Basically he designed the new wing as a barn or music-room, including a large open fireplace with ingle-nook seats, and log storage lockers. The wood-slatted roof was supported on some old oak beams from the old liner *Berengaria*, which was being broken up. To rest on this roof he had modelled a plaster cast of the Baden-Powell coat of arms and painted it in red, gold and blue heraldic colours. On the scroll below was inscribed the family motto: AR NYD YW PWYLL PYD YW – which means – well, what does it mean? 'Where there's a Powell there's a hole'? My father often wondered which was the true interpretation and whether the 'hole' was a pit of danger or a cave of safety.

Beyond the music room was my father's own study, with panelled walls, an alcove with shelves all round it and drawers full of all his fishing tackle – and a garden door to be used as his escape route into the rose garden should he not wish to be caught at home by an untimely visitor.

Upstairs he had designed bedrooms with windows down to floor level so that visitors could look out from their beds at the lovely view across the valley of the River Wey, southwards to Bordon and Hindhead. This was not a new idea to him. In South Africa long ago, he had suggested in the rebuilding of military hospitals that the windows should be so low that the patients could lie in bed and see what was going on in the outside world thus taking an interest in life instead of being left to die, staring at a blank wall.

The bathroom also came in for some of his artistic talent; all along the wall above the bath he modelled in plaster of Paris a bas-relief frieze of a river with fish in it, banging their heads on the bottom because it was so shallow, whilst on the river bank above them was a portly figure at a pump, drawing away all the water to fill people's baths. 'Why the Cochibondu is the water so shallow?' one beautiful speckled trout was complaining through a bubble above it. We were all encouraged to add our personal artistic childish contributions, and along the bottom of the river were painted rocks and stones, worms, crabs and tadpoles, such as our imaginations could manage.

When the new wing was completed, the initials of all the family were inscribed on a stone low down on the wall beside the steps from the garden door to his study. Each of us in turn had had a trowel thrust into our hands and had been helped to lay a brick. The initials of R.B-P, O.B-P, P.B-P, H.B-P and B.B-P are there as a permanent reminder of this little ceremony (though hidden now by a healthy growth of creeper) and of the happy family who once lived here.

7

The bedrooms of the new wing were kept mainly for visitors. We all had our rooms (each with our own choice of wallpaper) over the hall, the dining-room and the drawing-room, in the central part of the house. My father had his own special bedroom – the balcony from my mother's room. There he slept summer and winter, fair weather or foul, out on the balcony. He hated sleeping indoors, he said it gave him a cold! If the rain was blowing in he pulled a green canvas awning down from the wall and hooked it on to the wooden balustrade, as though he were in a tent. Whenever our parents were away we clamoured to be allowed to take it in turn to sleep out on the balcony. Jealously guarded memories could recall who'd had the last turn and we had to keep a strict rotation. Strict rotation too, for letting Winks in. Winks was an enormous tortoise-shell cat who slept out at night. In the early morning he came scrabbling up the creeper to one of our bedroom windows. Some beastly wire frames had been fitted to stop Winks getting in, but it wasn't difficult, as soon as he miaowed, to skip out of bed and bend back the wire to let him squeeze his way in and jump straight on to the eiderdown – muddy paws and all.

Apart from Winks, my father was the earliest riser. Every morning he carried out his ritual of physical exercises. He stood on the balcony, deep-breathing the fresh air, arms raised and stretching sideways and above his head; trunk turning and bending forward, knees bend and stretch. Then he came indoors, slipped into his Jaeger warm jacket and trousers (forerunners of the track suits of today) and quickly went down to his study to write at his desk. This, he declared, was the best time of the day for work, the mind fresh and clear after a night's sleep, the house quiet, all peace and silence with no distractions, and overnight problems having been slept upon. Besides, there was an apple awaiting him. It was the parlourmaid's duty, the evening before, to leave on his desk a dessert plate and fruit. Nobody was allowed to dust the desk or tidy up the muddle of papers on it. It wasn't a muddle to him, he knew where everything was, and nobody else must disturb it.

Having achieved probably as much as two hours' work, he went back upstairs to join my mother making an early cup of tea or 'chota hazri' as he called it from Indian memory days. They made it themselves, they didn't like any of the staff to call them in the mornings, nor to run the bath ready.

At about eight o'clock, or three-quarters of an hour before the gong sounded for breakfast, they would be out of the front door, round to the kennels to collect the dogs and away down the drive. At the end of the drive they would usually turn right along the road to the Duncans' drive up to Coldrey, passing below the house behind its high yew hedge and along the farm road leading out on to the lane to Froyle and the Anchor Inn, exactly a mile away.

The dogs were Vic, an airedale who had superseded Jack (bought with the house), Taffy, a Welsh terrier and Estyn, a black cocker spaniel. At this time they were all strictly outdoor dogs who lived in a row of kennels with pens out in front like proper gun-dogs' homes. My mother used to love the back view of the dogs as they trotted on ahead of them, with neatly pointed back toes and the spaniel's floppy ears blowing back along her neck.

Nellie was the original name of the donkey who had come with her cart through the snow from Little Mynthurst to Pax. It was not long before we had her out of the shafts and B-P was helping us on to her back. She was so fat that she became 'Barrel' and when she became Barrel she was always referred to as 'he'.

Barrel didn't care for us much, when we were on his back. The bridle and reins made no difference to where we went, he was indirigible. Straight down the side of the drive he'd go and under an over-hanging laurel branch, so that the helpless rider was swept off over his tail. If that failed there was the high red wall along the path towards the village. He would scrape his fat side so close that the poor rider's leg was grazed or crushed. Further along, where vegetables flourished in cottage gardens, he would make his way in, regardless of agonized hauling on the bit, whip flailing and legs flapping, and start devouring cabbages. The only way out was when irate owners came running to the rescue, fists waving, to eject the helpless passenger on the destruction-bent beast of burden. They had to lead us out; we daren't dismount to lead him ourselves as he'd bite our legs when we tried to climb on again.

My debacle with Barrel came one hot summer's evening when the ground was very hard. He carried me smartly down a steep grassy slope into the rose garden and without any warning turned sharp right at the bottom. I went straight on, into a rose-bed, landing heavily on my left elbow, in great agony. My father, as ever, came to my rescue, noisy me, bellowing in wrath and pain. He comforted me and between sobs I was able to pull myself together enough to ask 'Do Brownies ever cry?' He thought they didn't usually cry if they'd hurt themselves, so I looked up at him, chin quivering, and tried to be brave as he carried me and my broken arm into the house.

In the garden, up beyond the green bank where I had fallen off the donkey, my parents developed a new herbaceous border. An ardent weeder, my mother's favourite pastime was 'standing on her head' digging up celandines. My father planted and trained apple and pear trees to grow fan-wise along wires behind the lupins and delphiniums and these he carefully pruned and labelled. Somewhere, in a gardening drawer, I still have the metal discs, oval-shaped, with 'Bon Chretien' and 'William' written by him in waterproof ink.

At the top of the grass path was the revolving summerhouse known as the 'Q.T. House' because it had been bought out of the proceeds of his military hand-book *Quick Training for War* which had been published in 1914. Here he could go and work or rest in solitude and for two summers we children, with Penny, our sporting governess, used it as our outdoor classroom. It had camp-beds and rickety tables and folding canvas chairs called 'Rawkees' and it was a delightfully distracting sort of school-room; all the dogs and the cat, Winks, joined us there and lay about on our books.

Round the walls were four long brown boards, Rolls of Honour with all the names of all the horses my father had ever owned written in bold black lettering. These were fascinating and much more important to learn by heart than 'Hail to thee blithe spirit', much more interesting than trying to digest another page of *Piers Plowman*. We would try to commit to memory BUDDEROO and TANCRED, OLD DUTCH and CRUSADER while we watched the clock for lunch time when we joined our parents in the dining-room and could pour out a torrent of names and ask Dad to recollect stories about TIT WILLOW, MISCHIEF and MOSQUITO. These latter had been his polo ponies in Malta when he had been stationed there in 1890 as Military Secretary to his uncle, General Smyth. ACONITE and BULAWAYO were chargers he had had in South Africa; another one, with a long, ugly body, he had called TOU-LON and a troop horse with C.4 branded on his hoof he named SEAFORTH. In India he had had two grey polo ponies, SPECIAL and GREY EARL whom he'd taught to come to his whistle and they followed him around the cantonment like dogs. His most famous pair were HAGARENE and PATIENCE, his brave pig-sticking mares, each of whom had won him pig-sticking cups (tales of which shall be related further on).

The last names on the board were ORARA and BLACK PRINCE (initials forecasting Olave and B-P). These two were magnificent-looking chargers given to him after the siege of Mafeking by the delighted people of Australia. They were sent across to South Africa to be presented to him but by the time their ship arrived he had already left for England and so they were despatched on another sea voyage to follow him there.

After he retired from the army to start the Scout Movement B-P thought he had no further use for the horses so he gave Orara to his friends the Halahans to hunt in Lincolnshire and Black Prince went to Lucy Kemp-Welch, the well-known horse artist, as her model. He was the model for her illustrations for Anna Sewell's epic book, *Black Beauty*, as well as featuring as the officer's charger in her famous Royal Artillery painting, *Forward the Guns*, which was hung in the Royal Academy in 1917 and now belongs to the Trustees of the Tate Gallery. The last time my father rode this horse was when he accompanied King George V at a parade being held at Windsor in the year 1911 and they rode side by side into the Great Park to inspect a Rally of Scouts assembled there.

Now, a decade later, we children were beginning to clamour for something more than Barrel to ride. So Black Prince came out of retirement and spent the last few years of his long life helping us to learn to ride. We couldn't climb onto him by ourselves, he was over seventeen hands high, but we sheltered under him, we said, when it was raining and also he would put his old head down low while we sat astride his neck (facing the tail) and then he would toss us up onto his back. Also he would give us swings; with our arms clasped round his neck he gently raised and lowered his head, his eyes nearly closed in silent tolerance as he swung us off our feet.

To save Black Prince having three of us riding him together, another old friend was acquired through the auspices of the Home of Rest for Horses, a black pony called Toppy, in size midway between Black Prince and Barrel. A splendidly ill-assorted trio they were and with this little troop assembled, as well as the dogs, it wasn't long before our parents made time from their work to take us out for 'walk-rides'.

Despite the number of working hours the B-P's put in at their desks and the unceasing journeys they made to every county in the British Isles, addressing meetings and forever encouraging the growth of the Scout and Guide Movement, they always seemed to have some time to play with us. My father had a ready response to the excuse which people so often made – 'I haven't time'. 'Haven't time,' he said, 'You have all the time there is!' And if people said that Scouting was impossible for them, he replied that 'Nothing is impossible, except putting tooth-paste back into the tube.' He certainly practised what he preached, for he somehow managed to devote time to us and we were able to spend many happy hours with him.

He loved being out-of-doors as much as possible and led us off for walks through the hop-fields which surrounded Pax. In summer-time – and it always seemed to be summer-time then – he was dressed in khaki shirt and shorts and an old straw hat with an Old Carthusian ribbon. Grasping his thumb-stick and summoning Taffy with a cheerful call of 'Here boy', off we would go down the kitchen garden and under the pear tree pergola where my mother tied little muslin bags on to each pear to stop the wasps from stealing the fruit. A high privet hedge on a bank formed the boundary of Pax garden and there was a narrow green door, overgrown with ivy, which we children couldn't open, the latch being too high up. 'Watch what Taffy does', my father taught us, as the Welsh terrier leapt up the bank and disappeared through a hole in the hedge. So we followed, scrambling after him and wriggling through the gap on our tummies. 'Don't make the hole any bigger', he would warn us, putting the twigs back, 'in case others might discover your secret way and use it too.'

This garden door led out on to a footpath which is part of the old Pilgrim's Way, running from Winchester to Canterbury. The footpath ran more or less parallel with the main road between Alton and Farnham, passing through farmland where hops were grown. Acres of fields were occupied by rows of tall poles linked by strands of wire with strings stretched from ground level to the topmost wire for the hop vines to wind their spiral way. Much of the Hampshire countryside around here and north and southwards between Basingstoke and Petersfield was an important hop-

growing area and the first touch of autumn came round each year when we heard the low hum from the old kilns and sensed the sulphurous smell wafting on the air at hop-drying time.

When the gipsies arrived with their long-tailed skewbald horses and their round-hooded caravans, they were given accommodation in long low wooden sheds. However, most preferred to stick to their own in the fields set aside for their encampment where they could sit around their campfires as dusk fell, their horses standing like tethered sentinels on an outer circle.

Mrs Wade described the countryside so much better than I can in a poem written in 1933 entitled 'Our Own Bit of England':

I will not sing of the Surrey hills,
Of neat little houses with snowy frills;
Of lawns cut close and drives swept clean,
For the millionaire with his limousine.

But I will tell of the Hampshire side,
For Hampshire houses are old and tried
And Hampshire country is much the same,
As in the days when the Pilgrims came.

Now, half a million eggs, they say,
Are sold in Alton on market day,
And Hampshire hops make Alton ale,
As fine as any in song or tale.

If ever you tire of suburban towns,
Just breathe the air on Holybourne Downs;
At Cuckoo's Corner the wild birds sing,
To pilgrims weary of wandering.

The step of the tired wayfarer quickens,
By the scarlet blinds of the 'Hen and Chickens',
And past and present meet in the tale
Which is told round a barrel of Alton ale.

Have you watched the kingfisher fill his bill,
When the sun is shining at Isington Mill?
Where under the bridge across the Wey,
Are brown and speckled trout at play.

Many a waggoner ceases toil
At the friendly gates of 'The Anchor', Froyle,
And drinks to the pungent smell of the hops
Which grow in the fields round Coldrey Copse.

Away to the north, behind sheltering yew,
Is Mary's Church, which the Pilgrims knew;
Where folk like us, full of joys and cares,
Have worshipped God for a thousand years.

To Bentley Green at close of day,
Boys and girls come out to play;
Nor ceases the knock of bat against ball,
Till the stars shine out and the nightjars call.

South, overlooking the Holt, there stands
The ancient fastness of Marylands,
A rosy castle of youthful dream
Keeping guard over forest and stream.

If your day must end with a final pull,
You may choose the 'Star,' 'Red Lion', or 'Bull',
For the 'Bull' is the last of the wayside inns,
Where Hampshire ends and Surrey begins.

CHAPTER THREE

1925-26

A glass coffee-making machine with spirit lamp sat on a little table beside my mother at the far end of the dining-room table and B-P had his place on her right hand; between them the waste-paper basket. The post had already arrived by breakfast time, the letters being delivered to the front door by an exhausted postman with a large canvas bag on the front of his red bicycle.

The letters were opened and envelopes discarded, but not before the stamps had been saved. These were a geography lesson in themselves and were eagerly sought by such stamp collectors as Mrs Wade's small son, James (one of Dad's many god-sons), or put aside in a bowl on Mum's desk for future distribution to appealing small collectors.

Mrs Wade arrived at breakfast time, sometimes on foot from Ash Cottage, sometimes in Jimmy, her little Standard car. ('I will send my little *cat* to meet you at the station' she had once erroneously typed to an important foreign visitor arriving at Bentley.) She came with her shorthand notebook and her despatch case filled with letters for signature. To my mother she was always 'Eileen', to my father 'Mrs Wade', and she sat by the window, pencil and notebook poised ready to help deal with begging letters, awkward ones, appeals, requests for messages, invitations, bills, receipts, bundles of papers from Scout and Guide Headquarters in London, all requiring attention, consideration and replies.

Ignoring the choice of dishes on the sideboard – poached or scrambled eggs, kedgeree, mushrooms, bacon or sausages – my father most enjoyed a light diet of stewed fruit at breakfast. Also he liked very thickly cut toast so that he could split it open and put the butter in the middle. We children would come in (often a little later) and lift the silver covers off the dishes just to see what lay beneath but declined most of them as none of us were large breakfast-eaters. My father always had the most diminutive helping. 'He has the appetite of a fly' my mother said despairingly as she tried, unnoticed, to slip another poached egg on to his plate. Coffee was drunk from very large, steep-sided cups of blue and white Delft china with

Ewhurst Place

Heather Grace.
June 1st 1915.

Lady Baden-Powell
returns thanks for
kind enquiries and congratulations.

Ewhurst Place.
Sussex.

Peter and Teddy

Great-Grandfather, Admiral Smyth

___MY ARRIVAL___

St James's Church, Ewhurst, 13 July 1915

Aunt Connie Smyth, Godmother

Matthew Hale, Godfather

Ewhurst Place, 13th July, 1915.

PROGRAMME.

2.30.	Scouts parade in troops on Rectory Lawn.
2.45.	Scouts march in troops to line road near Church.
3.10.	Chief Scout and Lady Baden-Powell pass.
	(Troops Salute)
3.20.	Scouts march by troops to Ewhurst Place, and line drive and roadway.
3.40.	Chief Scout's party returns.
	(Troops Salute)
3.50.	Whistle Signal - one long blast - Scouts take cover as directed.
4.0.	Whistle - one long blast- Rally to lower lawn.
	Troops come to the Alert smartly - SILENCE - Salute the Flag.
	Tea on lower lawn. Patrols light fires.
4.30.	Bands play alternately on the lawn.
4.45.	Displays- selected from

Rye	Emergency 1st Aid.
Northiam.	Ambulance.
4th Eastbourne.	Ambulance.
1st Eastbourne.	Maze Drill.
Polegate.	Field Extension Drill.
Wadhurst.	Single-sticks.
Sandhurst.	Club-swinging.
Hawkhurst.	Pyramids.
1st Ewhurst.	Sketch.
2nd Ewhurst.	Whistle Drill.
Roedean G.G.	Tent Pitching.

5.45.	Chief Scout inspects Troops.
	Whistle Signal - one blast - Scouts form a hollow square in troops.
6.0.	Scout games - blindfold boxing etc.

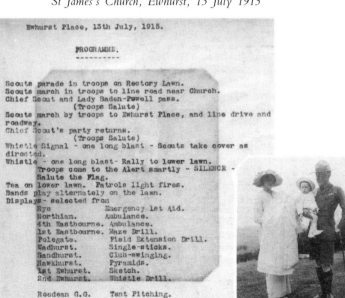

Edith McConnell, Godmother

AND CHRISTENING

equally deep saucers; a beautiful crocus-like Minton design.

Not only at breakfast-time, but often at lunch as well, Dad would bring forth little yarns, ditties and doggerels. Inspired perhaps by a foggy morning, he would start off with

I had a piece of string
Quite a tiny little thing
Tied as tightly as a string should be
But a fellow in the fog
Came and cut away the dog
And I've nothing but the STRING *you see.*

He might also relate (in an Irish brogue) the tale of the mother summoning up her courage at lunchtime to break the news to little Sheenagh that her dog had been run over:

'Sheenagh,' she said quietly, 'I'm afraid Paddy's dead'. The child looked pensively at her plate for a time, then looked up and said 'I think I'll have some more puddin'.' Greatly relieved that the news had been received so complacently, the mother gave her more pudding. Later on she heard dreadful tantrums, crying and wailing from outside, and a sobbing, desperate Sheenagh came and hurled herself into her mother's arms, moaning 'Paddy's dead, Paddy's dead'. 'I know, I know', said the mother comfortingly. 'I tried to tell you so at lunchtime.' 'Och,' said the child, 'I thought you'd said Daddy.'

If it wasn't the day for an Irish story, there was a favourite 'French' chant:

Oh Jean Baptiste pourqoui
Oh Jean Baptiste pourqoui
Oh Jean Baptiste
Oh, why did you grease
My little dog's nose with tar?

Your little dog had a catarrh
Your little dog had a catarrh
He cough and he sneeze
So that's why I greased
Your little dog's nose with tar.

Oh Jean Baptiste c'est bon
Oh Jean Baptiste c'est bon
Oh Jean Baptiste
I'm GLAD *that you greased*
My little dog's nose with tar.

Or perhaps we might be treated to a 'German' recitation of the Lorelei, sitting on her rock where 'ruhig fliesst der Rhein'. 'Ich weiss nicht was soll es bedeuten, das ich so traurig bin' and as she was combing her golden hair, each verse he would end with the line 'Dad Madchen mit nottings on'.

If all was silent at the meal he would suddenly grimace and, looking very uncomfortable, would cautiously put a finger to the corner of his mouth, eyes shut, head inclined. Then, with a pursing of the lips and a quick grab with finger and thumb he would catch the end of an imaginary hair. Gradually he would start extruding it from the corner of his mouth. Longer and longer it became, so that the other hand would have to come up and help. When he'd 'got it out' he started winding it round finger and thumb, then quickly rolled it up into a ball – and popped it back into his mouth. Tongue in cheek (metaphorically as well as literally) he held it there. We loved this act. Again and again, bobbing up and down in our chairs, we'd call for repeat performances.

'I wish I were a little rock', he'd start off in a high thin falsetto voice, to the tune of the well known hymn 'O God our help in ages past', and gathering volume as he continued with us in chorus, the last line ended with a shout:

> *I wish I were a little ROCK*
> *A'sittin' on a hill*
> *A'doin' nothin' all the day*
> *But just a'sittin' still.*
>
> *I wouldn't eat, I wouldn't sleep,*
> *I wouldn't even wash.*
> *I'd just sit there a thousand years*
> *And rest myself – BY GOSH.*

Nothing drove my mother more quickly from the dining-room table than when he embarked upon 'Love's Golden Dreams'. With hands clasped over her ears she fled to her desk in the drawing-room, knowing this lurid reminiscence of a voyage to Australia when their cabin was situated between that of an opera singer (Melba) on one side and a sea-sick traveller on the other.

This was a sort of running commentary on what he heard:

'Love's golden dreams are o'er' practised the prima donna, rejoined only too realistically by somebody being violently sick. 'Hidden by mystic dreams' trilled the singer, before another awful rendering of retching from the sea-sick cabin interrupted again.

Of all these chants and ditties I think our favourite was the recitation of 'The Scarecrow'. This verse would be recited first in the voice of a peremptory colonel, snapping out commands, then in the pious voice of the vicar, and then of a local yokel and finally repeated in the piping nervous little voice of a small child who goes so far and then can't remember the next line, pauses, thinks, goes back to the beginning, rattles through the lines, comes to an abrupt halt and after vain attempts to end it all, bursts into paroxysms of tears.

THE SCARECROW

> *I stood on the swampy field of battle*
> *Of skulls and bones I made a rattle*
> *To frighten away the carrion crow*
> *And the homeless dog, but they wouldn't go.*
> *So away I fled for how could I bear*
> *To see them gorge their dainty fare.*

Until they realized that he was playing the part of

himself as he thought he ought to appear at his age, the unwary breakfast visitor could be startled by Dad's sudden announcement – 'England is going to the dogs . . . and these fellers have no idea how to govern . . . Now when I was in India in '76 . . .' So convincing was his impersonation one could readily be taken in as he transposed himself to a London club where he was angrily reading the leader of *The Times* while complaining to the waiter about the toughness of the steak or to his neighbours about the state of the weather and the imbecility of the Government, interspersed with wheezy clearings of the throat, splutterings and loud 'damns'.

In yet another act which brought breakfast-time visitors to their feet he would pretend to be leaving the room and as he was doing so he would kick the bottom of the door with his foot, then turn into the room again clutching his nose and with a grimace of extreme agony and his nose all bent sideways he would sit down again to be soothed by all the people who'd been taken in by him.

After an unhurried breakfast their work began again as they went to their separate desks, my mother to her typewriter in the drawing-room, to deal not only with Guide affairs but with household matters as well; my father, followed by Mrs Wade, went through to the seclusion of his study. The study was furnished in his favourite colour scheme, long grey velvet curtains and a 'raspberry mousse' coloured pink carpet covered with a zebra skin and in one corner a lion skin with the head

mounted on a stand. The walls were wood panelled on either side of the fireplace and in the far corner, on a pedestal, was the bronze bust of the bearded Captain John Smith which he had sculpted in 1907 and which was then exhibited in the Royal Academy. Captain John Smith was one of his historical heroes and he always maintained that the Smyths in his family's forebears were descended from this character. Smith was one of the early settlers in America and founded the State of Virginia and he married (though this is sometimes denied) Pocahontas, the daughter of a Red Indian Chief. Dad's sister, Aunt Agnes, tried to find out more about him and this is what she wrote to us shortly before she died:

As to Captain John Smith, he had no children that we know of, but the Smyths may have been related to his 'family' as shown in their armorial bearings. This spirited filibuster fought in any war that was going and when there was war against Turkey he dashed off there. He chopped off three Turks' heads in one morning and when he returned to London Queen Bess awarded him three Turks' heads as his coat-of-arms. Our great-grandfather, Joseph Brewer Palmer [note the B.P.] Smyth had these arms on various of his possessions, as also had our grandfather, Admiral W.H. Smyth. You would learn all this in that fat little book of Captain John Smith which the Chief Scout was very fond of. . . . [But where is that fat little book?] Unfortunately, our great-grandfather was drowned in a ship-wreck when coming home from America and his widow and little boy knew nothing about his Virginian connection. This is all rather vague as I can only remember being told it as a child.

With a morning's work done, my father would lean back in his swivel-chair and rub his hands together. This action was a characteristic expression of pleasure and satisfaction of a morning's work achieved and a load off his mind. He had dictated letters to Mrs Wade and handed bundles and sheaves to her, on which he had usually scrawled a few words of action to be taken. Letters signed, completed and put into their envelopes were tossed to the floor with a satisfied thud.

One day I can remember him registering particular hand-rubbing pleasure at the end of the morning. The *Discovery*, the renowned ship in which Scott had made his first voyage to the Antarctic, had been advertised for sale. Moored in the Thames, wouldn't it make a splendid Headquarters for the Sea Scouts? But how to acquire it? How could the money be raised? To whom could he appeal? He took a piece of ordinary 'Pax Hill' headed writing paper and wrote to 'Dear Lady Houston' and then drew a most superb pen and ink sketch of the *Discovery* in full sail and explained the circumstances. How could this lovely vessel be left to go to the breaker's yard? Could she not be preserved? Would it not be an opportunity for posterity . . .? He was genuinely pleased with that drawing and later had even

greater satisfaction with the result, for there came an enormous cheque from Lady Houston with which to buy the vessel outright, moored at the Embankment, as he had visualized, as the Sea Scouts' Headquarters.

He also quoted to us another incident involving Lady Houston. When he was boarding a night train to Scotland he stepped into what he thought was his sleeping compartment, only to find a lady undressing. 'So sorry, sir,' he politely improvised as he backed out again in confusion.

Apart from his happy hand-rubbing gesture, Dad used to whistle to himself too. He had two types of whistle; a happy contented sound, sort of hissing through the teeth like grooms make when strapping horses in the stable, and another louder whistle which implied that he had got to a difficult place in his work. 'A Scout smiles and whistles in all difficulties' he had written as part of their code – and he never preached what he did not practise. My mother could whistle a little bit too, but with her it was always the same tune – 'The Sands of Dee' and only the first four bars of it anyway.

With a load of work cast aside onto Mrs Wade he would leave his study and come, hand-rubbing, into the drawing-room where my mother would immediately drop her work to find out what he was planning to do. They each called the other 'Dindo' and my mother also called my father 'Robin', abbreviated to 'Bin'. 'Bin' he always signed himself in all his letters to her, and to her only. If he really wanted to catch her attention he would call 'Harriet' in a pre-emptory but joking tone, for she had once declared that *that* was a name she was glad she did *not* have.

My mother wrote everything on her typewriter, rarely anything by hand (only condolence letters, or to us children on our birthdays). Her hand-writing being large and laborious was not fast enough for her thoughts and couldn't keep up with her. Her typing could keep up – but only just. Seeing that she had taught herself entirely and only used what we derisively called the 'Hunt and Peck' system, it was amazing to observe the pace at which she went. Often she would gallop off into capital letters, forgetting to press the shiftlock down again. Very expressive typing it undoubtedly was, with uneven margins, double, sometimes treble spacing of lines, many delightful spelling mistakes (wrong letters used in right places) and well punctuated with exclamation marks and ¾ instead of full-stops.

Each week she typed programmes in duplicate or triplicate for the household staff, copies being distributed to the kitchen, to Bear and to the housemaids, stating what was happening each day; by which train my father would travel to London, which car she would want ready to drive herself to Foxlease, the new Guide training centre at Lyndhurst (for we had Jim-major now as well as Jimmy); when to take us children to our (dreaded) dancing-class; who was coming to stay and for how many nights; which bedrooms were to be made ready; who and how many for dinner on Wednesday – all times and details precisely given. Consequently, how smoothly the household ran.

During the winter months the Pax Sketch Club sprang into being, usually for half an hour on Wednesday evenings. My father 'took the Chair' – his wing chair by the drawing-room fire; the rest of the members, and any visitors staying, sprawled about on the floor as near to the hearth as outstretched dogs would permit. Armed with drawing-pads and pencils we awaited the announcement of the subject; each week a different member had to declare his or her choice. 'A Frosty Morning' was ordered and off we'd go, heads down, bottoms up, pencils (and rubbers) busy; and sometimes, if enthusiasm waxed strong, paint boxes were brought in, mugs of water and much sucking of paint-brushes to make a fine tip. Mugs could be overturned onto the carpet by a dog's limb suddenly outstretched or by a foot from a near-by competitor.

'Don't go over the edge' my father cajoled as he watched and encouraged us to paint a 'masterpiece'. My mother took no part as a competitor; she either sat in a corner of the sofa darning socks, with a large wooden mushroom rammed into the heel, or she remained at her desk, playing 'background music' to us on her typewriter, keeping up with her Guide correspondence and running the affairs of the house.

On some evenings the Sketch Club exchanged drawing pads, each member making a squiggle or shape from which, when handed back, the owner had to form a drawing. When our time limit was up we all exchanged drawings and by everyone initialling on the back the one they thought best (I think my father's entries were *hors concours*) a winner was declared. It was noticeable that my father's initials were usually to be found on the back of the sketch least likely to win – just to give a little encouragement.

Sister Betty once drew a tiny dog looking out of an enormous kennel when the given subject was 'Too big for him'. I'd painted a horse looking at a high post and rails fence and B-P had sketched a man wearing a top hat coming right down over his ears.

Sometimes, on Fridays, Mrs Wade didn't come; the early morning walk was shortened and my father would be dressed in his dark brown suit ready to go to London. Bear brought the car round from the garage, backed up to the front door and stood holding the car door open. My father, with bowler hat and umbrella, stepped in (front seat of course, he always sat beside the driver) and away he went to catch the 9.25 a.m. from Bentley station to the City, because Friday was Mercers' Day.

Having been 'born' into the Worshipful Company of Mercers, my father carried out his membership duties fairly regularly, especially now that he had a settled home, not far from London. Courts were held on Fridays and these he attended as frequently as possible, particularly when he had duly taken his turn of office as Master of the Company during the years 1913–14. Sometimes the meetings of the Court must have dragged on a bit, but my father's wakeful eye was watching fellow members as they nodded off and his ever ready pencil caught them in their somnolent postures. Alas, during the Second World War the magnificent Mercers' Hall in Ironmonger Lane was reduced to ruins when it received a direct hit during a bombing raid on London. How sad my father would have felt had he known, though happily now a phoenix has risen from the ashes and a new building has restored it to its former glory.

On arrival at Waterloo station, my father would slip along through the crowds, out of the folding gates of the platform and down into the 'Drain' – the underground line to the City. His underground reconnaissance was remarkable; it was difficult for a child to keep up with him for he would dart down turnings where it said 'No Entrance' and come out just ahead of everybody else.

As a treat on some occasions I was taken to London too, especially if he was bound for the Scout Headquarters. These were fine premises with a shop, well sited in Buckingham Palace Road, just opposite the Royal Mews. Whilst Dad was conferring with various personalities such as 'Pickie' (Sir Alfred Pickford), Dymoke Green, Godfrey Fausett, Hubert Martin and other Scout Commissioners, I was allowed to go and sit in somebody's office, nose pressed to window, hoping to see a royal horse come out of the Mews. Sometimes I was lucky, as pairs of Cleveland bays going out on exercise, put to a drag, with liveried coachmen in top hats with cockades would come spanking out under the archway and merge into the stream of traffic towards St James's Park.

The most memorable trip to London with my father, was my first visit to the Zoo. I wanted to see the jackal which some Canadian Scouts had presented to brother Peter during the Wembley Jamboree but alas it had died in the meantime and he was compensated later when given the pelt. So, no jackal, my father took me off to see the chimpanzees. They were so funny, swinging about from the top of their cage and stretching out their long arms, asking for nuts or sitting wisely contemplating their own finger-nails; blinking solemnly and then suddenly swinging away and hanging upside-down by their tails, or sitting and scratching under their arms – so appallingly human I thought they were, I was doubled up with laughter, so hysterical that a crowd gathered round, no longer looking at the animals, but at me, crying with laughter and oblivious of the onlookers.

Exhausted, we caught the train back to Bentley in the darkness. My father relaxed and dozed in a corner seat and I sat opposite to him, back to the engine, anxiously watching as we drew out of Farnham and rattled on into the night. Would he wake up soon? Did he know that Bentley was the next stop? Should I tap him lightly on the knee? Had I better rouse him from his nap? Oughtn't I to climb up on the seat and get his bowler hat out of the rack? What will happen if we get carried on to Alton?

All was well as we gently screeched into Bentley, the solid figure of Bear standing in the shadow of the dim platform lamp, ready to escort us over the iron foot-bridge, through the ill-lit little station and out to the waiting car. 'Je suis dos,' Dad would announce cheerily in his best French as we came in through the glass doors of the hall at Pax. Anybody questioning his command of a foreign tongue would be offered the test of how to translate 'Would you please put your umbrella down'.

At Pax animals came and went, as animals are wont to do, weaving their way into our hearts. Jack, the airedale, had perished. (Morbid little children, we'd crept round behind the garage to watch Bear bury him on the rubbish heap.) He was replaced by another airedale, Vic; Taffy, in his turn, was succeeded by another of my father's real loves, a little Welsh terrier called Twm, given to him by the Copelands when he was on a visit to the Potteries in Staffordshire.

Black Prince had also 'gone to his happy hunting ground' so we'd been told. In his stead there came a pony called Dido whom none of us particularly liked; all too frequently her head went down between her knees and we went over her ears. My father, however, picking us up for the umpteenth time, said cheerfully, 'If you want to be good riders you must fall off at least eighty times.' Once we realized there was no stigma attached to falling off we sometimes rolled off on purpose. What a ghastly fall Betty had once when Dandy crossed his feet while cantering down a plough furrow and she went headlong into the newly turned earth. I got off my pony quickly to help pull her to her feet and anxiously wiping her face which was plastered with mud I asked 'Are you all right?' And there came the reply, 'That's SIXTY-EIGHT'.

Dido achieved fame in one way when featuring in the local Press at a meet of the Hampshire Hunt at Bentley Station. Great excitement as my parents dressed us all up, dumped us on the shaggy ponies (two children to each pony, Peter and Betty on Toppy, cousin Yvonne and me on Dido) and led us, rather fearful but at the same time very excited, to the Meet. There, in the conglomeration of horses and hounds, bicycles and foot followers, were some anti-blood sports agitators and in the papers next day headlines reported 'Chief Scout teaches children blood sports' with a picture of a terrified pair of little girls clinging to Dido's back, facing firmly in the opposite direction to the hounds.

The cutting from this paper went into a file my father kept entitled 'Pats and Pinpricks'. There came through the post one day, however, an item he couldn't get into the file; it was a black cardboard model of a coffin, in which he was told he could bury the Scout Movement.

Summer-time riding was the best of our fun when very often in the evening my parents, having done a day's work, would leave their desks and we could all sally forth on our favourite 'walk-rides' – ponies, dogs, parents and children would set out in single file through the rookery, across the stubble fields to Froyle. Following 'up-and-down' lanes and footpaths, round to Isnage and Well, past the Lillywhites' farm and Bentley Church lane, we came back along the path behind Jenkyn Place, skirting the hop-fields, to Pax. On our assortment of fat ponies we were sometimes sent on ahead as scouts to spy out the land, counting how many cows or sheep in a field, what dogs or cats belonged to which of the cottages in Froyle. Using our powers of observation we had to notice the mileages on signposts, how many ash trees in the hedge between here and the Crondall turn, or where was the nearest oak tree.

We came bustling back to make our reports and scored points for recounting all we'd seen. Rather out of breath, bringing ponies to attention (we scored points for a good, square halt), we saluted, then gave a concise report to the Inspector (without letting the pony nuzzle for sugar or start nibbling grass). He returned our salutes, announced our scores and then sent us off again. How many elms between here and Isington Mill? How far is it from the bridge to the Binsted fork? Such good walkers were my parents that on these rides six to eight miles was considered 'just a nice walk-ride'. As I.G. on the Continent, B-P had observed how far behind were the Cavalry in Britain compared to the Cavalry on the Continent. He realized there was a need for dressage, so he started the School of Equitation at Nether Wallop, later transferred to Weedon. In the preface to her book *The Story of Riding*, Mrs E.N. Kellock wrote: 'He did so great a service to British equitation'.

With enough ponies to go round, Barrel was relegated to the shafts and became the centre point of all-day ride-and-drive excursions to Frensham Pond. With my mother at the helm, the cart or trap was loaded with picnic baskets, bathing towels and even a tent (for in those days one concealed oneself to undress on the sands). Off went the cavalcade, down towards Bentley station and under the railway arch, along the edge of Alice Holt Forest, up to Bucks Horn Oak, across to Dockenfield and, crossing the bridge by Frensham Mill, we came out onto the sands surrounding Frensham Ponds.

My father usually joined us later in Jimmy, the two-seater car with a 'dicky' back, and helped us to off-saddle the ponies and strip ourselves for the delicious moment of running into the water. We led Barrel and the ponies in too and they enjoyed it as much as we did, pawing at the water and splashing us and even wanting to lie down and roll.

Tuesdays were ruled out for riding, as Scofield needed Dandy for the mowing. Dandy was put in harness and with enormous leather boots strapped to his feet, he plonketed up and down the lawn. 'Don't hinder the men' we children were told as we were seen slinking off in the direction of the garage yard. We loved to go and 'help' to clean out the blades of the mower with garden knives; or we would pretend to be sweeping up the yard and would occasionally find ourselves (accidentally?) soused with water as Bear was hosing down the cars.

Moon daisies – tall white marguerites – grew in profusion all along the banks down to the lawn. When they were in full flower, the entire staff from Scout and Guide Headquarters were bidden to come and spend a day at Pax. In bus-loads they came and the event was spread over two days so that the London offices didn't close down. My parents wandered about chatting with them all. They were given food and drink and could wander at will through the house and garden, browsing over scrapbooks, pictures and trophies from every part of the world. The ice cream man, with his 'stop-me-and-buy-one' bicycle combination, was also invited and served out ice creams to anyone who wanted them, the bill coming in next day to the hosts. When evening came, the visitors clambered back into the buses, their arms full of moon-daisies and their minds full of lasting memories.

Pax also kept its doors open to welcome and revive acquaintance with groups of people brought together after many years of having lost touch with one another. By dint of judicious research, the 'boys' who had attended the experimental Scout camp my father had tried out on Brownsea Island in 1907 were traced and invited to lunch. When they arrived they were 'organized' to sit together in their original patrols of twenty-one years previously – the Curlews, Ravens, Bulls and Wolves. Sadly their numbers had been depleted by the 1914–18 war and in every patrol there were gaps with only the 'gone home' sign beside the name. One day in May we children had been occupied in the schoolroom writing out, in our best script, menu cards to be put on the table for a big lunch party. This was a gathering of the people who had been in Mafeking in 1900 – either in the siege itself during those seven long months, or who had come in the Relief Column which had reached Mafeking on 18th May to set them free from the Boers.

Momentous gatherings of many other old friends were held and they all had a wonderfully evocative time 'do-you-remembering'. What sanguinary names we seemed to hear them mention! We overheard tales of such 'knights' as Sir Bindon Blood and Sir St. John Gore. We learned also about the 'fierce exterior' of Sir Baker Russell, commanding the 13th Hussars when my father first joined the Regiment which was then known as 'The Baker's Dozen'. 'Up till noon he was a devil' ran the reputation of this fiery colonel, 'and after noon he was an angel'.

Pax was not the only scene of these friendly reunions. Frequently my father found himself journeying to London for Regimental Dinners, Old Carthusian Meetings, Old Comrades of the Cavalry and nearly always, as Guest of Honour, he was called upon to make a speech. Speech-making came naturally to him, his subject was at his finger-tips and he was never at a loss for an amusing tale, often with a dig at himself. He did not have to refer to notes and he could pitch his voice so clearly that he had no need to shout, nor did he like a microphone. At out-of-door Scout rallies and huge gatherings such as Jamborees he was expected to use a loudspeaker or tannoy, but he hated having to resort to them and always referred to them as 'these damned contraptions'.

Besides official dinners there were also many very formal day-time functions, such as Levees in full dress with medals, and the Royal Garden Parties at Buckingham Palace. It was just as he was leaving one of these state parties that he overheard an exhausted guest moaning, 'My shoes are tight, my corsets are tight, my husband's tight and I'm going home.' On another occasion my parents were on their way to Buckingham Palace when the car had a puncture on the Hog's Back. They flagged down a motorbike and sidecar and were taken to the gates of the Palace. Dad, in his full levee dress, arrived at the doors still clutching his gardening gloves.

CHAPTER FOUR

1926-29

To my father's regret, but by Nature's course, we were growing older and he missed hearing the run-about feet in the nursery or the clattering on all-fours, playing 'horses' up and down the landings until our knees were pink and sore. We now walked solemnly, sauntered even. The nursery had become up-graded to a schoolroom, with exercise books and copies of *Child Education*. Governesses had replaced nurses and we moved about as disciplined young people. We thought about playing tennis, riding bicycles as well as ponies and Penny, the governess who came after Gam, even tried to teach us to play the piano. Such was her teaching enthusiasm that, to encourage our progress, we had to give concerts at the end of each term. The concerts were held in the music-room, with parents for audience in the front row, on the leather sofa, and a few of the household staff dragged in to sit awkwardly at the back. We handed out schoolroom-made programmes; the curtains were drawn, table lamp angled on to the music rest; last minute whispered instructions from Penny before Betty and I were settled at the piano to strum out our favourite duet, Sehnsucht's Waltze; or she would play her party piece and sing 'Lavender Blue, dilly-dilly, Lavender Green'.

I wasn't trusted to sing a solo. I used to play 'Thuringian Air' (blurdging through the trills) and then had to face the audience to recite Kipling's

They shut the road through the woods
Seventy years ago
Weather and rain have undone it again
And now you would never know
There was once a road through the woods. . . .

Together we would sing, to Penny's accompaniment, the Christopher Robin song:

Half-way up the stairs
Is a stair where I sit.
There isn't any other stair
Quite like it.
It's not at the bottom
It's not at the top

But this is the stair
Where I always stop.

Sighs of relief when the programme came to an end, some polite hand-clapping, kisses from our parents and everybody filed out while we blushingly put the music-room straight and drew back the curtains.

The music-room was used not only for concerts; in winter holiday time it was the ideal playroom on dark evenings for us all to play 'Giants'. Lights out, we groped about amongst the furniture, round the piano, brushing past the floor-length curtains trying to rescue the 'prisoner' from the giant's den under the seat in the big bay window. Luckily it was a fairly quiet game, not disturbing my father, if he happened to be working in his study next door.

One evening a week the room was cleared of furniture for Country Dancing; it became a craze which went on into the summer-time too, and people came in their cars from round about for regular Country Dancing sessions. We learned the movements of several dances set out in Cecil Sharp's book, with the tunes on gramophone records, played on our old 'growler' standing in the corner where somebody had to keep winding it up.

We learned the steps of 'Rufty-tufty' for two couples, 'Hunsdon House' and 'Goddesses' for four; 'Gathering Peascods', 'Sellinger's Round' and 'If all the World was Paper' for a circle of people dancing into the centre and back. For this last one we chanted:

If all the world was paper
And all the sea was ink,
And all the trees were bread and cheese
What should we have to drink?

My father used to come and join in, especially for a little foursome called 'Parson's Farewell' which we all enjoyed because of the funny little nod the dancers made to each other at the end of every movement. All the time he was dancing, Dad was whistling the tune to himself.

In 1926 another pressing call came to my parents, to come and help give direction to the Scout and Guide (Pathfinders) Movements in South Africa, and a heavy itinerary was made out for them. They decided, instead of compressing it all into a couple of months, to extend it by including a visit to Southern Rhodesia and, in between, to take a month's holiday at the Cape. Best of all, they decided to take their children with them!

We had a lovely sea voyage to Cape Town and there we were put into schools while they carried out their official tour. Peter went to Bishop's at Rondebosch, Betty and I to St Cyprian's, on the slopes of Table Mountain. Here we slept in large, cool dormitories, for it was coming into summer-time in the southern hemisphere in October. We learned to play Hopscotch in the sandy open quadrangles surrounded by white cloisters and red-tiled roofs. Our eyes goggled at the mounds of Hanepoot grapes put before us at meal times. We ate grapes and half-moon slices of pink watermelon every day; nuns flitted about and conducted us to the crypt for prayers and some days we went for walks up in the forest on the mountain-side, gathering up pine cones, picking out the 'donna-pits' and nibbling them as we walked on over Kloof Nek. Other days we were taken to the sea-filled swimming pools at Sea Point, returning to school by a tram which rattled its way up the streets of Cape Town.

Came the Christmas holidays and reunion with parents and Peter, when we spent a whole month at Gordon's Bay, hardly ever getting out of our bathing suits. We had a bungalow practically at the water's edge, facing across the bay to the Cape Peninsula and here we ate and slept and swam and my parents were able to rest and relax before the second part of their tour.

'Come on', my father would call to us, as, at seven o'clock, the sun rose over the mountain behind our bungalow and shone on some rocks at the water's edge. 'You can't lie there all day like hogs in clover with the sun scorching your eyes out.' We rolled out of our beds where we slept out on the veranda or stoep, and trotted down to the sea for our morning bathe.

Along the shore and following sandy paths up the slopes covered in Protea bushes we collected and learned the names of many South African wild flowers, including the orange and white chincher-inchees; and my father painted views of the Hottentot Hollands, of the vineyards at Meerlust and Vergelegen and sketched the local characters as they went about the village of Gordon's Bay.

Home again from South Africa, the open arms of Pax awaited us all. Back to the schoolroom for us girls whilst Peter, following in Father's foot-steps, went to Charterhouse – not as a Gownboy or in Duckites as my father had been, but in Saunderites, one of the three Houses forming the main block. He enjoyed being a Carthusian and made many friends but achieved no distinction in any way, except to play the part of 'B-P in Mafeking' in the Masque which was performed once in every four years. But neither had my father had a distinguished career at school, apart from playing in goal for the First XI. When he pulled out some of his old school reports to show to Peter, he decided to put them away again, for the 'beaks', or masters, had written such comments as 'Pays not the slightest attention' and another wrote 'Seems to have given up all interest in this subject'.

Peter was still a 'new hop' when my parents were included amongst a host of illustrious guests bidden to be present at the opening ceremony of the new chapel at Charterhouse, designed by Gilbert Scott. When surreptitiously asked what he thought of this fine piece of modern architecture, my father was heard to murmur 'It would make a good hangar for an air-ship'.

Betty and I, hands clasped by governess, stood outside to listen to the service (if only I'd known it, my future husband, John King – also the son of an Old Carthusian and a future 1st XI goalkeeper like my father – was inside there, singing in the choir!) and then watched the trumpeters' fan-fare from the balcony high above the west door as the bishops and clergy came out in procession – crooks, mitres, copes, robes and all the panoply of the Church dignitaries.

'Let's combine business with pleasure' was my parents' solution to having to attend official functions during our school holidays. Thus started a sequence of summers when, with two cars, dogs, children and tents, they set off in convoy from Pax on camping tours. One August, for instance, we stayed the first night at a new Guide camping centre near Birdlip Hill in Gloucestershire, thence to Cardiff for a big Welsh Pageant and Rally and a trip out to sea in the Bristol Channel with the Sea-Scouts. My father, with Peter to accompany him, went on to carry out a Scout tour in Ireland while my mother attended meetings and Rallies in Wales and Shropshire. We girls stayed with relations in North Wales and prepared a camping ground at Wern where the family were all reunited. Most of our time seemed to be occupied in putting up tents or taking them down, getting soaked in rain or drying ourselves out, preparing meals and clearing up after them, some very chilly bathing in the sea, after which we came shivering back to camp, draped in gaudy-coloured towels and clamouring for mugs of hot cocoa or tomato soup. Peter wisely joined my father and off they went together to fish in a nearby lake instead of going down to the sea.

Fishing was one of my father's best antidotes to hard work. In his 'first life' – the military one – he had enjoyed sport, playing polo in India and Malta

and becoming one of the most renowned pig-stickers in Central India. Now, in his 'second life' he became a most enthusiastic fisherman. He had inherited from his brother Warington some salmon and trout rods and box after flat tin box of flies, ranging from the most gigantic and brightly coloured salmon flies down to the tiniest little dark gnats. And with Peter at his side as a willing pupil they would jog off together with the oft-repeated chant in their minds:

It's nice to sit and think and fish
And fish and think and sit,
And sit and fish and think and wish
The fish would bite a bit.

We continued our summer holiday through North Wales; we packed up our tents and bedding rolls, pulling the straps up tightly round the 'hold-alls' and, stuffing everything into the trailer and ourselves into the cars, we set out along the road again.

Bear drove one car, pulling the little trailer, and we three children bundled into the back of the other old Standard which my father and mother took turns in driving. We were disappointed that Snowdon was hidden in the clouds as we drove through lovely mountainous surroundings and past rushing torrents by Llangollen, Corwen, Pentre Voelas and on to Capel Curig. At Bedd-gelert we gloomily studied from behind iron railings the grave of Gelert, the faithful hound whom Llewellyn had slain, erroneously thinking he'd killed his baby son. We stopped again to gaze mesmerized at the Swallow Falls and later to walk up Miner's Bridge and then drive on by the Pass of Aberglaslyn. Then, heading south-eastwards for Dolgelly, Rhayader and 'Llandiddledoes', as my mother called it, we came unhurriedly back into England and pitched camp again at Kentchurch, the original home of Owen Glendower.

An amalgamated Rally for Scouts from five different counties had recently been held near Hereford and Colonel Sleeman, who had organized it all, had promised to give my father a Labrador puppy. We drove to his home at Hampton Bishop and as a bounding ball of black dog came rollicking across the lawn my mother, with her wonderful aptitude for naming things, said 'Oh, he must be SHAWGM,' explaining that the initial letters of the Counties concerned – Shropshire, Hereford And Worcester, Gloucestershire and Monmouth would make up this name.

Shawgm was my father's faithful black shadow for many years hereafter. Also he played a lively part acting as a salmon or trout when Dad went to practise casting a line on the lawn. As soon as he heard the rod being lifted down from its pegs, high on the wall of the verandah, he would leap to his feet and bounce round my father, then turn and dash on ahead, jumping down the banks and out across the lawn. My father then tried casting a 'fly' (but substituting a white pigeon's feather) and Shawgm would seize it up and tear away with it while the line screamed through the reel. Dad would play his 'fish' for a time, then quietly reel him in to his feet – perhaps to repeat the whole game over again.

Besides naming dogs my mother had given names to all the bedrooms in the house, and to the cars too. These latter all had to begin with 'J'. Following the original two-seater, Jimmy, came the saloon 'Jim-major' (who pulled the trailer, so that was named Jim-minor) and later there was a 6-cylinder Standard, 'Jim-max'. We were sometimes driven to London in Jim-max by Bear and he took us through the middle of Guildford instead of on the 'new' bypass so that we could wave to our dear old car 'BP', now standing on the taxi rank at the top of the steep hill up the main street.

It seemed to follow on naturally that when, on that memorable occasion at the Scout *Jam*boree in 1929 at Arrowe Park, Birkenhead, the Scouts of the World gave my father a *Rolls*-Royce, it instantly assumed a 'J'-name and what more obvious (having cost a few pence to any Scout who cared to subscribe) than 'Jam-Roll'.

This World Jamboree, which marked the twenty-first year of Scouting, should have been the culmination of my father's life work. But far from it! Although now aged 72, he and my mother (a mere 40), within the space of the next nine years, completed two world tours, a tour of Africa and then of India, not to mention lesser trips on the Continent, a Rover Moot in Switzerland, Jamborees in Hungary and Holland and three Cunard Line cruises with ships full of Scouters and Guiders. The great honour of a peerage, bestowed upon him at this Jamboree in 1929, he found most embarassing. It was only because he was persuaded to accept it, not as a personal recognition but on behalf of the Scout Movement, that he agreed at all. This recognition he acknowledged by including the name of Gilwell in the title, Gilwell being the Scouts training centre situated in the heart of Epping Forest, the hub of the spirit of Scouting.

He had looked for no recognition for himself; he had been most reticent about accepting the peerage at all; and how he winced when Bear, beaming with pride, held Jam-Roll's door open for him, saying 'Good morning, M'Lord'.

An example of my father's humility can well be illustrated by his attitude when having a meal at a restaurant. When proferred the menu he would never say to the waiter 'I *will* have' – but always 'May I have?' 'Anyway', he added 'it saves them the pleasure of telling you "It's orf".' His theory on going into a crowded restaurant, when you want to know which table will next be vacated, was: 'Look at the people's feet under the table. If they're well tucked in under their chairs, they've just come in, eating hungrily; but the one you want to get near is where legs are stretched out, they're leaning back, tummies full, feeling replete. They're the ones who'll be going soon.'

The aftermath of the Jamboree brought a spate of visitors to Pax. People from all parts of the world came to stay and were able to enjoy participation in the private lives of a 'typically English family.'

One of my mother's most assiduous hobbies was to keep scrap-books – great big oblong albums with interchangeable pages, into which she gathered Press cuttings, photographs, programmes, drawings, invitations, all in chronological order. Visitors had to sign their name and their country in the current scrap-book, and not only did she keep these up to date, 'spreading herself' as she described it, with her brush and tall jar of '20th Century' paste, at work with newspapers spread all over the drawing-room table, but she also kept albums for each of the children. Something must have been bred into us, for a habit was started which has not left us since, and scrap-books still go on in our families today. Squirrel-like, we collect and store up all photographs of favourite dogs or horses, cryptic messages on scraps of paper, pictures of friends punting on the river, eating in camp, cars we have owned and loved; race-cards, programmes, gilt-edged invitation cards, dance programmes that we used to be given with pencils dangling – all worthy contenders for the scrap-book collection.

It is not only the vice of scrap-book keeping that we seem to have inherited, but also the family disease of diary-writing. Daily reports on what's been going on *must* be recorded, not a day must be lost. Dull reading to an outsider they may be, being bare statements of each day's doings; no scandalous secrets of private lives, nor criticisms of other people's curious habits or how they conduct themselves – just straightforward entries, correctly, unemotionally told. Perhaps, as a sideline, a few world events might get a mention, such as 'Armstrong and Aldin walked on the moon'.

My father's diaries, now in the safe custody of B-P House in London, were usually embellished with pencil sketches and sometimes caricatures. He always caricatured himself either as a Scout or as a fisherman – and usually in a predicament. He did once write, however, that 'Caricaturing is not a safe game to play and I seldom indulge in it'.

During some of his long sea voyages which may have tended to boredom, indulgence sometimes got the better of him. On board ship, lying in a deck chair, eyes half closed or ostensibly reading a novel, he usually had a drawing pad to hand and couldn't resist temptation when some extravagant character walked by – a large-hipped woman in unsuitably tight slacks and high-heeled shoes – who would be fair game for his humorous pen.

CHAPTER FIVE

1929-32

September's first week-end was a date always booked in the parental diaries for 'Gilwell Reunion'. Anyone who had been to Gilwell and attended a training course there, attaining their 'Wood Badge' (two wooden beads on a boot-lace as a certificate), could come back for a week-end of revivification and nostalgia. Out on the camping field groups of tents sprang up, camp stores and canteens opened; people wandered round the huge camp fire circle, meeting old friends, shaking left hands and remembering occasions when Scouting took an active part in their lives.

My parents had their specially allocated camp-site, on the lawn out in front of the white house, the main building of Gilwell in those days, and we pitched our row of tents there. With the gift from the Scouts of the world of a caravan, 'Eccles', which Jam-Roll had to tow, our family camping expeditions had become far less laborious. My mother still had the 'Palace' tent (because it was so huge) which had originally been provided for the Prince of Wales (later the Duke of Windsor) when he joined in and camped at the Wembley Jam-

boree. It was large and white and cumbersome and needed all hands to help get it up; but my father (with Shawgm sprawled on the floor) could now enjoy the comfort of the bed in the caravan. Betty and I had green ridge tents from the Scout shop, classified as 'Scouters' models; Peter had the one called The Bulge and Bear camped beyond Jam-Roll in 'Old Leaky'. Jam-Roll, with a silver fleur-de-lys badge for radiator cap, was painted in the Scout colours of dark green with a thin yellow stripe, and Eccles was coloured to match.

My father laid out the camp kitchen. Camping 'gaz' had not crossed our path then, but there was the helpful contraption called Primus when a fire wasn't available, and a branch stuck in the ground served as a mug-tree. For meals we sat with our feet in a ditch against the boundary fence with the opposite bank forming an adequate table.

We children enjoyed it all, but much more did we appreciate the holiday when we set off to the west country, away from officialdom, my mother having bought tickets for the Military Tattoo at Tidworth. From Pax the little cavalcade went forth towards Andover and, nearing Grateley, began to watch out for a suitable camping place. Through some tall park gates my mother espied a lovely green field. 'Let's go in there' she said boldly and strode ahead to reconnoitre. The owners proved, as usual, to be old acquaintances (from Jamaica) and in no time we were lifting our tents out of Jim-minor and receiving orders where to make camp. Milk, eggs and fruit miraculously appeared from the lodge nearby and having set our 'house' in order, we snatched up rugs and torches and drove on to Tidworth in the gathering darkness. We could hear the distant music as we groped our way to the arena and crept into our seats in time to see the magnificent spectacle of the massed bands emerging through the woods and out on to the flood-lit parade ground. Headed by the drums and fifes and then Taffy, the regimental mascot goat being led in his gold-braided red rug, there followed the mounted bands of no less than three Cavalry regiments, the musical instruments and accoutrements of saddlery glinting in the searchlights. It was a thrilling experience for us of the young generation and a very moving occasion for my father, casting him back into his military life.

We were persuaded to pause a while in our camp at Grately and spent a day visiting Stonehenge, wandering as Druids between the giant monoliths and trying to grasp something of the mystical reasonings of the Trilithin dawn as it was understood by the sun-worshippers in building such a temple.

Jimmy Richardson, recently retired from the 13th Hussars, had invited us to go and camp on the downs at Manton where he was now in charge of a racing establishment with eighty or more racehorses in training. We peeped out of our tents on Dog Hill early next morning, grass wet with dew, to the sound of a sneeze and lightly stepping hoof-beats. The first string of young racehorses was filing out for their morning's work. Such large 'eyes' they had, with hoods on their heads and check-coloured sheets over their loins, and lads perched on them like monkeys, caps backwards, as they were let go in pairs to gallop some measured furlongs.

From Marlborough we moved on westwards to the Mendip hills where we set up camp for several days in a rabbity field sheltered by a belt of fir trees on Priddy Hill. We were led to explore Glastonbury, the 'cradle of English Christianity' and clamoured for woolly sheepskin slippers, here at this source of the wool industry. We came back through the medieval little 'city' of Wells, round by the cathedral to see the fine array of statuary on the west front, losing count of how many figures of saints there were. On the whole we were happier away from the man-made cathedrals and abbeys and preferred exploring the Cheddar Caves, Wookey Hole and the subterranean River Axe. Stalagmites and stalactites, dark grottoes and witches' caves held more fascination than craning our necks looking up at gargoyles, effigies of bishops and the statues of all those saints.

On our last day at Priddy something that was

vastly more exciting to us occurred than, say, the presentation of the freedom of any city. Our host Mr Tiarks came over whilst we were rolling up our tents and, pointing to a far hill, said, 'You see that pony up there on the other bank – well, you can have her if you can catch her.' My father was a little bit dubious, but that was how, in due time, Gipsy Moth was roped in and came to be another of the much loved creatures at Pax.

Eastwards we went, or westwards on alternate years on these 'Camping Tours', combining events of work and play, education and leisure. Some days we stayed around our camp, just enjoying the woods and fields and the outdoor life; other times we dressed up in our uniforms to go to official functions or big Rallies that had been arranged months beforehand and once there was the solemn occasion of the presentation to my father of the Freedom of the City of Canterbury and he was handed a very valuable gold casket.

The honours being showered upon our parents ('The Parentage' as we jointly referred to them amongst ourselves) we hardly understood and did not really appreciate, although we stood solemnly to attention behind them throughout the ordeals. The Parentage, though they worked so hard, always gave the feeling that they were enjoying it – as obviously they were – and Pax radiated an atmosphere of happiness. They were thriving on the satisfaction of seeing the Movements developing and spreading all over the world and sometimes they could justifiably pause, relax and enjoy their own home life.

Their days were filled with desk work and outdoor exercise and gardening. We children shared our darling ponies; beloved dogs now lived indoors and Shawgm had an enormous round basket on legs, made by the blind ex-servicemen at St Dunstan's. My mother always bought baskets in aid of this wonderful cause and the flower room was full of them, in all shapes and sizes. They were in constant use, sometimes for picnics and in the autumn for blackberrying, gathering up windfall apples and the carefully picked, muslin-bagged pears and for collecting early mushrooms in Mr Lillywhite's field over the stile beyond Pax garden.

Some evenings had their leisure moments with time for reading. The lower deck of the drawing-room table was laden with papers and magazines, predominantly the *Illustrated London News* and the yellow-bordered *National Geographic Magazine*. Of course there were Scout and Guide journals, too, in all sorts of difficult languages and the *Cavalry Journal* which my father had originally started. There were regimental magazines; the *Greyfriar* from Charterhouse; *The Scout* with Dad's weekly contribution and *The Scouter* with his monthly 'Outlook' on the first page. Perhaps the favourite of all was *Blackwoods* with its exciting world-wide stories which appealed to his love of adventure.

My father enjoyed reading whenever he had time for it and there was nothing he liked more than a good detective novel. How he would have enjoyed a Dick Francis of today. He was a great

Denis Wheatley fan and also derived much pleasure from the books which came out in the form of a typewritten file, with photographs on the front page of the contents of the murdered victim's pockets. Usually when he was reading a book that he had been asked to review he would read the right-hand page only – unless there was a particularly arresting situation, he said, which would compel him to read both. He thought it poor policy for the author to have a picture of himself as a frontispiece – as it might put one off reading the book. With winter coming on, my father declared that 'England is not a white man's country' and as this was the time of year when they were not being called upon to attend Rallies, Pageants or displays at home, they could pack their bags and be free to answer calls to distant (and preferably southern hemisphere) places. Within the next six years they completed no less than two world tours, one round Africa and one out to India, thus escaping several English winters.

Mrs Wade was always left in charge and all the responsibilities of Pax were lumped on to her shoulders. As we children were now away at school and could spend holidays with our guardians, the Thesigers at Liphook, Pax itself could be let for the winter months. Another headache for Mrs Wade was finding suitable tenants, but being so close to Aldershot it was usually possible to rent it to some homeless military people looking for a 'quarter' and it was thus that the Barnes arrived (and their daughter Catharine was born) at

Pax. Later on Sir Willoughby and Lady Norrie rented the house when he took up the appointment as G.O.C. Aldershot – and their baby son was also born there.

Pax itself also seemed to give birth to babies, for it has given its name to off-spring in many different parts of the world. Scout camps and Guide houses sprang up as the years rolled by and adapted the name 'Pax' with many and various suffixes, Pax Wold, Pax House, Pax Field and in translated forms, all taking their name from this one well-known house in a corner of Hampshire.

On their first World Tour – when they went left-handed round the world – my parents paid only rather a hasty visit to Australia, nipping through the Panama Canal and practically by-passing New Zealand. They spent most of the voyage at work on a sort of biography my father was writing, later published under the rather laborious title *Lessons from the Varsity of Life* – my mother hammering it all out on her typewriter in their top-deck cabin. I quote a letter I received when I went back to school after the Christmas holidays:

N.Z. Shipping Company's
RANGITATA
28th January, 1931

My very dear old Heatherum,
Tomorrow we expect to reach Colon Cristobal at the mouth of the Panama Canal. We shall pass through the canal and stop for a few hours

at the far end of Balboa, to take in oil fuel and then we start out across the Pacific for New Zealand.

I will post this to you at Balboa – though I have no news to give you because the voyage has been most uneventful. Fine weather all the way; only a small number of mostly middle-aged passengers. We don't know how many of them as yet because we have our own sitting-room cabin – *most* comfy – where I dictate and Mum types my new book every day and I think it will occupy us for the best part of this voyage. So that we are very comfortable and happy – except that I don't like being away from my dorters.

Never mind, I couldn't see you if I *were* at home as you are away at school. But as soon as you have done your schooling we will take some of these journeys together.

Indeed we will have a trip to the Continent in July, won't we, to see Chillon and Kandersteg. Only learn your French and German well meantime. Write and tell us all your news. Mrs Wade knows where to find us and will forward your letters on if you send them to her.

Your loving
DAD

It was while on this visit to Australia that my father met – and made note of – the ideal man to name as his successor as Chief Scout. The man whom he had spotted was Lord Somers, at that time Governor of Victoria. Great was his relief and pleasure when Lord Somers accepted his appointment as Deputy Chief Scout, but how tragically short-lived it proved to be, as he fell an early victim to cancer.

My mother also wrote us weekly letters all the time we were at school. No matter how busy they were, or in whatever part of the globe, we always received our typewritten 'portmanteaux', so-called because the letters contained everything. Carbon copies were sent to each of us, with little individual 'suit-cases' typed on the end. 'Dearlings', they usually began, or 'My dear Preciouses, all of you' and off galloped the typewriter with her inimitably expressive typing, with 'O' for 'I' and plenty of ¾ and ½'s for punctuation marks, describing where they'd been and what they were doing and also laying plans for where they would be moving on to next.

The most eagerly sought part of the letters to each of us was, of course, the answer to our questions – When would they be coming to see us at school? Would they come and take us out? Could we bring some friends with us? And will they *please* bring all the dogs.

As promised in their letters from Balboa, we youngsters were allowed to go with our parents to Switzerland during our summer holidays. Business combined with pleasure again, in the same way that we had enjoyed our family camping times in England. Our uniforms were an important part of our luggage and so was 'Beetle' my mother's little black portable typewriter. My

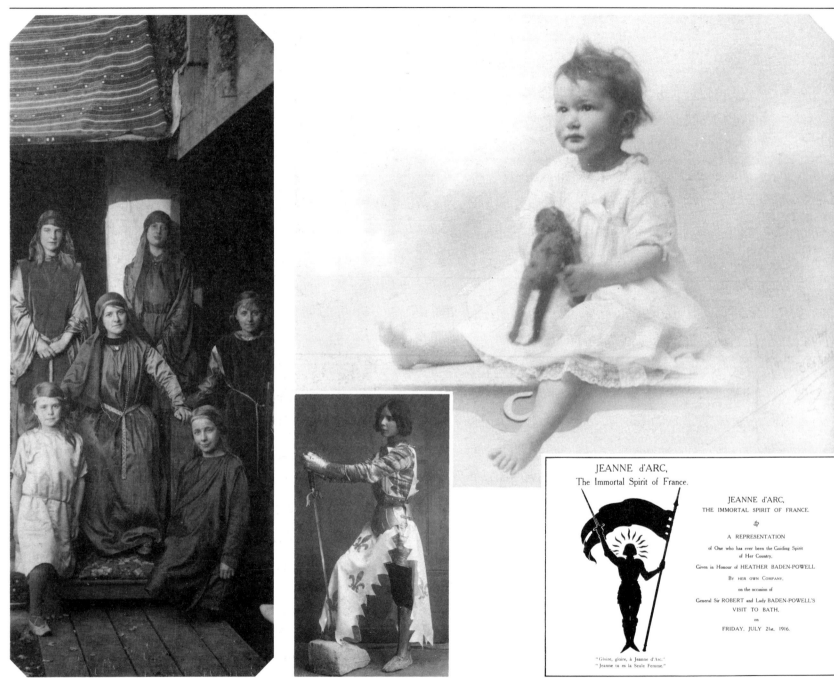

JEANNE d'ARC,
The Immortal Spirit of France.

JEANNE d'ARC,
THE IMMORTAL SPIRIT OF FRANCE.

A REPRESENTATION

of One who has ever been the Guiding Spirit
of Her Country,

Given in Honour of HEATHER BADEN-POWELL

BY HER OWN COMPANY,

on the occasion of

General Sir ROBERT and Lady BADEN-POWELL'S
VISIT TO BATH.

on

FRIDAY, JULY 21st, 1916.

"Gloire, gloire, à Jeanne d'Arc."
"Jeanne tu es la Seule Femme."

The 3rd Bath Company of Girl Guides perform a pageant for Mum and Dad after winning the distinction of the title of 'Heather's Own Company'

'HEATHER'S OWN'

R.B-P.

Dog for Heather

R.B-P.

LITTLE MYNTHURST

father had a suitcase called 'Blaster' because when Mrs Storrow had ordered it to be sent to him as a surprise present, on receiving it he said 'Blast 'er, it's the very thing I wanted'. My mother's suitcase, naturally, became Mrs Blaster.

We trundled out by train to Kandersteg for a camp gathering, 300 strong, of Rovers and Senior Scouts (now Venture Scouts). It was a 'Rover Moot', held in the beautiful Bernese Oberland, where there is a permanent international Scout camping place with a big chalet as a hostel.

'It was lovely,' I wrote in my schoolgirl's log-book, 'waking up in the morning and hearing nothing but the rushing of a great waterfall that comes tumbling down the mountain-side near to the Hotel, and looking up at the great mass of mountains, some with glaciers on them. They are glorious and one could just sit and stare at them quite happily all day. The trees on the lower slopes grow at such an angle that they must be very firmly stuck on; and the cows at pasture sound lovely as they move and ring their bells as though they were all going to church.'

We flung open the shutters and stepped out on to the sun-drenched balcony overlooking the Kander River, to join our parents at their morning coffee and stuff ourselves with croissants and black cherry jam. Scouts from several different countries had clubbed together to buy the big chalet when it came on the market. It had originally been built to house the people working on the Loetchberg tunnel and was abandoned when the tunnel was completed. It had taken six years to build this famous tunnel, all nine miles of it, under the mountains and round a glacier, to form a direct rail route straight through to Italy, from Berne to Milan.

The Guides of the world, rather like the younger of two little boys whom we knew, nicknamed 'What for?' and 'Me too', very soon found that they too needed an international chalet. So the following year we found ourselves lucky enough again to be travelling with our parents to Switzerland – this time to Adelboden. From Frutigen it was an exciting journey by 'Post Bus' up the valley next to Kandersteg and a stiff pull up to the beautiful new chalet. Hundreds of Guides from Britain as well as from many other parts of Europe and from all over the world were already assembled to see my mother officially cut the ribbon to open 'Our Chalet' as it is now known to visitors from all over the world. The site had been personally chosen and the plot purchased by a devoted American friend and benefactor, Mrs J.J. Storrow. Her late husband had been head of the Boy Scouts of America. We could remember her earlier visits to Pax when we were small and wondered why she always called my father 'Sir Rabbit'. This title soon deviated into 'Brer Rabbit' which he became to her and to many friends in the United States.

To return to England, the River Wey ambles along below Bentley – about a mile to the south – on its way from Holybourne eventually to join the River Thames at Weybridge. 'What a lovely little trout stream that would make,' my father once thought during one of our walk-rides over the bridge past Isington Mill. (The mill house at Isington later became the home of Field-Marshal Lord Montgomery, who died there in 1975.) We had found a grand occupation for ourselves in the summer holidays. Leaving our ponies loose in the Carters' field, we tore off our clothes and waded into the stream, pulling out dead branches, up-rooting some of the rushes and reeds and having many a lovely wet, muddy hour or more clearing the banks where they broadened out below the bridge. Putting the proposition forward to a few local friends and the riparian farmers owning the river banks, my father soon found that the Bentley Fly-Fishing Club had sprung into being.

To stock the river, a lorry from Hungerford brought tanks of small fish from a trout hatchery. As we 'helped' to release them into the stream we found that some of them had fainted on the journey and had to have air breathed into their gaping mouths – they were given the 'kiss of life' before they were lowered into the water and wiggled their way up-stream. An old Bentley resident can remember how, as a small girl afflicted with polio, she would watch for my father's arrival because he would lift her in and out of the stream, telling her to catch some 'worms' for him to fish with. He never could resist having a laugh and a game with small children.

Scouting was certainly not his sole occupation in life and he always advocated that the more one could bring in from outside, the better would be the work for the Movement. But he looked upon a day's fishing as the 'fee' he was entitled to for a day's scouting. He lived out of doors for as many hours as he could and the hours he gained from each day by working a two-hour shift before breakfast, he reckoned earned him an extra month in every year of his life.

He was never idle; that does not mean to say that he was restless, but he always had something on hand he could turn to. He could be found painting or drawing and had recently taken to sculpting again. In the alcove in his study he set up a modelling table, as he had in mind to design a symbol of chivalry for the basis on which to build the Rover Scouts' initiation and training. He modelled a knight in armour, kneeling at the altar steps, helmet at his side, offering up his sword in out-stretched hands. (Most of the time the out-stretched hands were offering up a spatula or other of his modelling tools.)

I loved watching him at work, picking up a bit of clay myself and rolling it in my fingers. One day, after he'd been to London, I found a little modelling table standing beside his, and on it a wire skeleton armature; and after some length of time I found I'd made a model of a rearing horse!

CHAPTER SIX

1933

Repeatedly in his letters, as I was nearing school-leaving age, my father made light-hearted references to his need for a 'dorter-secretary'. 'Mrs Wade may be run over by a bus any day', he said – not only once but so often that Mrs Wade began to take this possibility as a probability and to train an assistant in her office at Scout Headquarters. Looking back on it now, years and years later, I can see – with a good deal of self-recrimination – how much more I could have helped, instead of gadding off to stay with friends for dances, going out hunting on Gipsy Moth, and, evening after evening, going out to the Cinema.

However, I was anxious to learn and to try to pull my weight; so, with the assistance of Jummy, the baby Austin, I 'jummied' five miles into Farnham every morning to the Commercial School of Shorthand and Typewriting. Here we were taught the hieroglyphics of Pitman's phraseograms, contractions and grammalogues as well as learning rhythmically, with the aid of a metronome, to use the typewriter. The keys were covered over with little black caps so we had to raise our heads to look up at the letters on a chart on the wall and never were we allowed to use a rubber.

At home I tried to pick up a few wise secretarial tips from Mrs Wade although I could never hope to aspire to her heights of efficiency and capability from her long years of inner knowledge and understanding of the way Dad worked. Nor was I of much use to my parents next winter when they included me on a visit to Malta and thence to Rome – I left the typewriter behind!

A week in Malta included some nostalgic moments for my father, having served there in the capacity of Military Secretary to his uncle, Sir Henry Smyth, in 1890, some forty-three years previously. Apart from attending to the immediate present – the salute of a great gathering of Scouts and Guides on the Marsh race-course, with Colonel Worrall (dubbed Colonel 'Worry-all'), the organizer, anxiously watching threatening black clouds – we were able to go delving back into the past.

By bumpy roads between high stone walls we

drove out to Tarxien to creep about amongst the Neolithic temple remains and down into the Hypogeum where Druids used to worship. Dad directed the driver to come back by a steep hill climb up into Citta Veccia, the old capital of Malta, to see whether the St John's Cross, carried in the Crusades, was still kept safely in the cathedral.

Back again in Valetta he took us to see what kind of office accommodation was provided for the Military Secretary of today – and there we found the same desk that he had had specially made, a high one, sloping like an architect's drawing-board. But now the comfort of a high stool had been added.

When Dad was Military Secretary in Malta he hadn't really enjoyed the official functions, least of all the social parties at Government House. On one occasion he thought he would enliven the rather dreary reception and so told a fellow aide-de-camp that he had something else to do first and would come in later. But would he, the A.D.C., please look out for an Italian reporter who had been bidden and be specially kind to him and see that he was introduced to His Excellency, as it was important that a good impression should be made in the Italian press. Off went B-P to his room, dressed himself up in his Italian reporter's disguise and duly handed in his (self-issued) invitation card at the door as he made his entry to the reception. He was met, as requested, by the very attentive A.D.C. who made a great fuss of him and, speaking excruciatingly bad French (for he knew no Italian), escorted him around and introduced him to many guests. Before reaching the Governor himself, however, B-P became so convulsed with laughter at this treatment that his mirth reached a pitch where great tears were rolling down his cheeks. Seeing the look of consternation on the A.D.C.'s face, he cried 'I sink I go; I feel a leetle bit seek in zee eyes', and, mopping his face, he bolted from the room. Quickly he changed into his high-necked uniform, stood up straight and came back into the midst of the reception in time to hear all the twittering that was going on about the extraordinary little Italian guest. An agitated A.D.C. grabbed B-P by the arm and was trying to explain the sudden disappearance of the Italian reporter when the hideous truth suddenly dawned – he noticed that B-P too was 'a leetle bit seek in zee eyes'.

From Malta we journeyed on to Rome where my father had, on the same day, two very important engagements and on the next day a very interesting tea party. The first was an audience with the Pope (Pius XI) to seek his blessing on the Scout Movement from the Roman Catholic viewpoint, as he was anxious that they should not split into separate organizations. For this occasion he had to wear evening dress (which was rather confusing as it took place in the morning) and my mother had to wear black from head to foot, not revealing any part of herself and even putting a veil over her face. The Charge d'Affaires, Mr Kirkpatrick, helped with this 'fancy dress' and borrowing Mrs Kirkpatrick's long cloak to shroud her own evening dress we wrapped her up in gloves and shawls and bundled them off to the Papal Palace while Mrs Kirkpatrick took me for a walk through the Villa Borghese.

The second 'audition' was an equally ceremonious affair, being with no less a person than Signor Mussolini, Il Duce himself. It was known how unapproachable he was, but my father sought an interview with him in order to try and glean more information from him about his new 'Balilla' and 'Avanguardisti' Movements. Having read B-P's handbook *Scouting for Boys*, Mussolini had incorporated many of its ideas and was now using them as a basis – though military – for the training of boys, forbidding Scouting (being a voluntary Movement) throughout Italy.

We had heard tales of how he received people for interviews, sitting at the head of a long narrow hall, glowering over his desk and summing them up as they approached. 'A man's personality is visible in his appearance', Lady Kennet, the sculptress, once wrote as she scrutinized characters she was about to portray. Mussolini was obviously making observations along these lines too.

I have in my scrap-book, in his neatly-pencilled hand-writing, my father's account of this interview:

On 2nd March [1933] the British Ambassador, Sir Ronald Graham, took me to see Signor Mussolini. He lives in the great palace in Rome which was formerly the Austrian Embassy. A small entrance, with a sentry at the door under the archway leading to an interior court or garden with tall palm trees. Footman received us with Fascist salute, right hand held up at arm's length. We waited for half an hour in the ante-room with fourteenth-century pictures.

Mussolini's room was a great bare marble hall – with no furniture. Walls painted to represent pillars, etc. In the far corner a writing table and reading lamp and three chairs. The Duce awaited us there and came out a few steps to meet us, speaking fair English. Small, rather stout, in morning dress but genial and human with a low, soft voice, not a bit the bombastic or commanding figure one had expected.

He sat us down and after a word or two of his admiration for the Boy Scouts I said I had come to pick up hints from the Balilla and it had been arranged that I should see them tomorrow. Also I was interested to hear how he made the working man take healthy exercise and play outdoor games. This was said to be voluntary but I could not see how he managed to make them all take it up, to the extent that innkeepers complained of loss of trade. He put his hand over his nose and stared hard with the whites of his eyes showing (a favourite way with him) and said, as he lowered his hand flat on to the table 'We do it by MORAL force'. Free passes on the railways, cheap tickets to entertainments and various privileges of that kind to those who go in for sports – until it has become the 'Thing'. This, coupled with drills, and exercises and uniform-discipline of the

Balilla, will make the next generation a fine, manly race.

We had about ten minutes' talk and in saying good-bye he accompanied us across the hall to the door.

The third event of this memorable visit to Rome was the invitation to tea with Signor Marconi. It was a charming and informal affair and his hand-written letter from the Senato de Regno, in completely colloquial English, welcomed us to his house. 'Our address is 11, Via Condotti', he wrote, 'and our dwelling just across the courtyard.' There we were entertained to tea by his wife and their little child of two-and-a-half, who was soon to be found sitting on Dad's knee.

Radio was an invention so new to us then; we had hardly progressed beyond the 'cat's whisker' stage. We had what we called 'The Wireless Set' in the barn at Pax and sometimes clustered close round it to listen to the News. My father turned it on very rarely – and equally infrequently did he ever use the telephone. The telephone lived discreetly in a little room to itself, beyond the green baize door. Tall and black, with the receiver hanging on the hook at its side, it stood on a low shelf to which was drawing-pinned a typewritten list of local numbers and there were doodlings pencilled round and round the drawing-pins. Bentley 8 was our number in those days and Mrs Wade was Bentley 2.

We children often closeted ourselves in the telephone-room, ringing up and arranging things with our own friends and it was also a medium for saying 'Thank you'. From an early age it must have been impressed upon us that we should either write or telephone to say 'thank you' for things we had been given or had enjoyed doing. 'Nothing is yours until you have thanked for it' was a maxim that was dinned into our dear little ears.

I had rather a tearful thank you letter to write after being taken to Aldershot to be shown Carclew, a famous pig-sticking horse which Colonel Scott-Cockburn had brought back to England from India. He had won the Kadir Cup with him no less than three times (to win it once is the height of any hog-hunter's ambition). I sat down to write my childish thank you letter; I knew how to spell 'Carclew' all right, I'd seen it over the stable door, but oh dear, great tears welled up – however do you spell 'Kernel', and, even worse, 'SCOTCOBUN'? As usual there was a loving father to go to and I picked myself up off the floor (we always wrote letters lying on the floor) to join him at his desk where, picking up a fat drawing pencil, he spelt out the mysterious words for me to copy and soothed me out of my predicament.

The year 1933 was particularly hectic for my parents – my diary shows just how hectic it was. By road, by rail and by ship (but mercifully not yet by air or they would have had no respite at all) they were travelling constantly in the furtherance of the Scout and Guide Movements. My father was now seventy-six and no wonder that, by the end of the year, he became tired and ill. Despite my mother's entreaties to 'Go and rest, darling',

BUCKINGHAM PALACE ROAD,
S. W. 1.

HEATHER POTTY POO
DADDY LOVES YOU.

WHEN HE COMES BACK
FROM FRANCE

BLACK PRINCE WILL START TO
PRANCE

BUT HEATHER WILL NOT
CARE

SHE'LL STILL BE SITTING
THERE

Because SHE WILL HAVE A
LOVELY SADDLE TO RIDE ON
IF SHE IS VERY VERY VERY
VERY VERRY
GOOD !

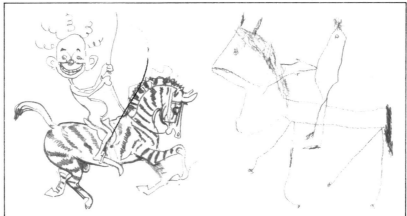

R.B-P.   October 1919   H.B-P.

H.B-P., 1922

My very first horse, 1917

On Barrel

With Barrel, Toppy and Black Prince

FIRST HORSES

ER ROOCK SITIN ONNA TRE

A rook sitting on a tree

Pax Sketch Club, 1923

With Nursie, 1922

Dad and Taffy

DADPOT REEDING PEETURS LETUR

ER PIDJIN SITIN ONN ÆR STULE

A pigeon sitting on a stool

Scofield

With cousins Clare, Yvonne and Christian

Picnic – and Barrel

CHILDHOOD

he only partially submitted. He would take himself to lie on 'Healer' (from Heel's the furnishers, of course), the chaise-longue which he wheeled out into the rose garden for a while, but before long he had pulled on his old leather gloves and with the secateurs from the garden-room drawer, would be pruning or dead-heading the roses or cutting out the cheeky young suckers.

He could rejuvenate himself with the ever-refreshing fishing, although my mother rarely accompanied him. There was the oft-quoted time when they went off to Wales to fish on the Wye and she elected to stay in the car while he went down to the river. He took a whistle with him so that when he got into a salmon he could blow for her to come and help him land it. He did get into a fish and he blew and he blew and he *blew* on his whistle. But she didn't come and she didn't come and eventually he managed to beach it by himself. When he carried his prize back up the bank to the car she was filled with surprise and delight – but why had she not heard his frantic whistle? She had brought her portable typewriter in the car and was clattering away at her letters!

Fishing was really my father's best antidote to work but riding he could no longer enjoy. Occasionally he would get on one of our ponies to ride with us but he confessed that he didn't really enjoy it any more because it 'gingered up' an old injury of a bullet-wound through his knee. Also he had been having some back trouble, described loosely as lumbago. This reached peak agony when he – taking Peter along with him – went off to another world Jamboree being held in mid-Europe, at Godollo in Hungary. He didn't mind riding slowly, or being on a quiet, obedient horse which would stand immobile when hordes of cheering Scouts rushed towards him and he liked to ride through the camps so that they could all see him without jostling him and he could see them well too.

But there came the Opening Day when Admiral Horthy on his high-tailed Arab led him a sharp gallop right across the parade-ground to inspect the Scouts lining up for their March Past and then another smart canter over to the saluting base right in front of the crowded grandstand. By the time they reached there he was too stiff to get off the horse and had to have several people to help him down. This caused considerable adverse comment in the Press, although once he reached the dais he managed to stand there for over an hour, watching and waving to a flowing river of Scouts, from twenty-three different nations, as they gaily marched by.

CHAPTER SEVEN

1933-34

If you build Castles in the Air, your labour will not be lost – that is where they should be. Now put the foundations under them.

This was exactly what my mother did. She dreamed castles in the air of taking a whole ship-load of Scout and Guide leaders, sailing from Britain, to visit Scouts and Guides in other countries. She dreamed of it when she herself was visiting a delightful Guide camp at Bucze in Poland and thought how lovely it would be if lots more people in the Movement besides herself could come and see.

'Do it now,' my father replied to her suggestion. 'If ever you have a good idea, do it now!' So off to Cockspur Street she trotted, went into the offices of the White Star Line (as it was then) and said boldly, 'I want a ship.'

'Yes, Madam,' said the polite young man over the counter. 'Where do you want to go?'

'Oh, to lots of different places,' she said airily, 'but I'll need a whole ship.'

Somewhat non-plussed, he referred her to the manager who ushered this impetuous person away into his office. The result was that, after giving her name and explaining the motives of her request, the following summer a whole liner, with 700 Scout and Guide passengers and a few friends and relations, set sail from Southampton.

They went to Rotterdam then eastwards through the Kiel Canal and cruised all round the Baltic capital cities, returning by the Skaggerak to Oslo and thence to Liverpool, a round trip of some 3,500 miles. At each place they were welcomed, entertained and received into the homes of the Scout and Guide people of those countries. They were taken in bus-loads through the country-side, shown museums and churches, statues (mostly nudes in Scandinavia!) and old historic buildings as well as the new. There was a river trip on the Vistula and motor-boat trips round the Swedish islands; we visited Scout and Guide camps on lake shores and amongst the northern pine woods, with tents nestling in clearings in the forests and 'gardens' made in the sand. Rallies were held on Baltic sea-shores and we were received or farewelled on cobbled quay-sides with bands and music and singing and waving, many amongst the crowds dressed gaily in national costumes.

On the last evening on board ship, the Chief Scout gave an address to the whole ship's company at a 'Scouts' Own' service, at which he said – in a voice so strong, his power of oratory so moving:

. . . On this tour we have seen for ourselves a small part of what our Movement has done among other people. This has been a very happy cruise where we have seen strange lands and have come face to face with Nature at her best in the sunshine, in the calm seas, in the beauties of the countries, of the forests and the mountains, of the waters and the sunsets we have seen. We cannot help feeling that the God of Nature has been with us. And then we have met our foreign brothers and sisters – unlike ourselves in many ways, unlike each other even in these neighbouring countries, speaking different languages, having different customs and different traditions, different histories and unable even to talk to each other, yet all united under the one ideal of love and goodwill. We have seen that for ourselves, we have felt it and we must realize that there is something behind us which is helping us forward – the spirit of Love.

Therefore I think we ought to pause for a moment in silent thanksgiving to God for having given us this happy outing, whence we come back refreshed and strengthened, I hope, both in mind and body; in thanksgiving for having found new friendships, new helpfulness, new experiences which we have exchanged with one another; in thanksgiving for fresh inspiration and new hope and faith in what we are doing; in thankfulness for having made friends of other nations who have welcomed us as we have welcomed them, new friends to whom we can be helpful by spreading the right ideas and right ideals of Scouting; in thankfulness for the privilege we have of helping, even in our small way, to develop that Love which, if it only spreads, will mean the reign of God upon earth . . .

Such a success had this cruise, this 'Argosy of Peace', proved to be (over-subscribed with more applicants than the ship could accommodate) that it was followed by two more within the next two years.

It seems clear now that these cruises, invented by my parents through a chance moment of enthusiasm (Do It Now!) sowed a seed in the minds of educationalists and were probably the fore-runners of the schools cruises of today. Previously, ocean-going cruises were limited by their price range, but these that my parents devised were much less expensive, being less luxurious and run rather on the lines of present day package tours, with a ship fully booked.

Wherever the ship docked, however, there were

ready-made friends, hospitable Scout and Guide people waiting at the quayside, with hearts and homes open to the visitors, to show them around and give them an insight into their own way of living. On board, also, there was much to do in the way of scouting games, competitions, country-dancing and reels, and programmes of events were drawn up for every day. Everybody was drawn into a Patrol and so mingled together for discussion groups, deck games and sorting out of social problems. Lectures were given on such subjects as 'Russia', 'The Baltic States' and 'Seabirds of the Arctic'.

Above all, these cruises gave to leaders and children alike in each of the places visited, the opportunity of receiving on their home ground these two legendary figures, the Chief Scout and the Chief Guide.

The beginning of the year 1934 must have been awful for my mother. On New Year's Day Betty was sick at breakfast and decided she didn't want to go hunting on Dandy. Two hours later she'd had her appendix out in a nursing-home near Farnham. The very next day my father had to be driven urgently to Sister Agnes' Hospital in London for an operation he had been trying to stave off for some time. Peter was packing up ready to depart to Rhodesia and I had gone and got myself (unsuitably) engaged.

I don't know how she endured those long weeks when my father lay in hospital, his life in the balance. She made daily journeys from Pax to

be with him; he was recovering from the first part of the operation, although suffering awful moments of pain, and within three weeks was able to withstand the second part. There was an agonizing forty-eight hours of suspension between life and death when my mother was allowed to stay in the hospital and be at his bedside, but at last we were told 'He's safe', and my mother came away for some sleep. Then two days later she received a telephone call while we were lunching at the Rubens Hotel (where they always kept a room reserved for her) to say that he'd had a relapse and a haemorrhage and was being given a blood transfusion. He had a good night after that and was making a remarkable recovery, chatting with the nurses and saying he was so pleased with the new blood that a donor Scout had given him!

By the beginning of February the bulletins were good, he was having good nights and was making rapid progress. At the end of the first week of February there came the day when my diary stated, 'Mum stayed at home all day as Dad is so much better' and there was talk about bringing him home by ambulance. Then sickening news came through again; he'd just had his tea when he had another relapse and drifted off into unconsciousness after another blood transfusion. Miraculously he pulled through yet again and from then on he improved daily. 'Coming on nicely' came the report, and next day, 'Going on splendidly, sitting up in chair'.

Mum continued journeying back and forth most days but sometimes we stayed in London to

see a play to cheer ourselves up. We saw *Fresh Fields* – very funny with Ellis Jeffries and Lilian Braithwaite as sisters; *The Sleeping Clergyman* and *Laburnum Grove* with Ralph Lynn, Tom Walls and Yvonne Arnaud.

Then came the joyous evening at Bentley station where I was waiting for Mum returning on the evening train. She burst out with the news 'He's coming home on Thursday!' He was brought gently home from hospital in a large Daimler ambulance, accompanied by Nurse McGahey. He arrived very cheerfully and was taken to bed in the big bedroom in the guests' wing of Pax (with the windows down to floor level as he had designed) as he couldn't be allowed back on to his narrow balcony bed yet. Gradually his old strength and vitality were coming back to him – though the twinkle and sense of humour had never left.

The first Scout and Guide Cruise had proved so popular that another was already steaming up for the Easter holiday period, this time southwards to Gibraltar and into the Mediterranean, though alas not including Italy, as Scouting had been abolished there, superseded by Mussolini's Balilla. At first it had been thought my father would not be well enough to go on the cruise at all. His doctors, however, finally acquiesced and he was given their permission to go, provided, Scout's Promise, he never left the ship at any of its ports of call. He agreed to abide by his Scout's promise and so, with 'Nanny' McGahey in constant attendance and our own local doctor, Dr Hussey (whom he

teasingly called Dr Fussey), as a passenger, he was practically carried on board. By mid-April, when the cruise-ship *Adriatic* docked again at Liverpool, he was able to walk jauntily ashore, completely revived.

The whole of the B-P family had been together on the first of these cruises the year previously, but the second one didn't have Peter on the list – he had gone forth to Southern Rhodesia. Although my father managed not to show it outwardly, he had been deeply disappointed, when Peter left Sandhurst, that he had shown no inclination to join his old Regiment, the 13th/18th (by now amalgamated) Hussars. This disappointment was short-lived however, when, after an interview with the High Commissioner for Rhodesia, Peter was offered the chance of joining the B.S.A.P. and this he readily accepted. Originally raised by my father at the end of the Boer War, this was a Civil Force (initially called the South African Constabulary) set up to replace the Military. With the maintenance of peace as its main objective, he was well content with his son's chosen career.

With Peter thus established, Dad recovering from his illness, and Betty leaving school and joining me at the School of Shorthand, the year 1934 suddenly brightened up again for my mother. In mid-summer the fishing-rods came out again and Dad swept me away to the River Deveron for a fortnight's fishing in Scotland. He could see that the best way to help me disentangle myself from my wrong love-life was to disentangle my fishing-line from an overhanging tree! How clever of him; it did the trick and at the end of October we happily stepped on board the *Orama*, each parent with a secretary-daughter in attendance, eastward-bound for Australia.

The main objective for this round-the-world journey was to be present at Melbourne in January for the first Scout Jamboree ever to be held in the Southern Hemisphere. It had been generally agreed that after Dad's recent illness, our parents should not embark upon these strenuous tours alone. It was providential that the Waltons were available and would accompany us, and we all went on board ship together. Granville and Joan Walton (extremely good at deck tennis) had long been associated with Scouts – he was Headquarters Commissioner for Rovers and she was well versed with the Laws of the Wolf-cub Pack, having run the village Cubs from their house near Abingdon. He was a bulwark of strength to my father, with his genial character, long cigarette holder, infectious laugh and a beginning-to-be-portly figure. ('He is practising Girth Control' it was reported in one of the Scout Jamboree daily rags.) He had an engaging manner of sidling up with some confidential observation which would be interspersed with light-hearted chuckles. We were a splendid team of travelling companions for the whole of the ensuing seven months and bonded ourselves together collectively as the 'O.P.' or Official Party.

We called in, on reaching the Mediterranean, at Toulon and donned our uniforms to go ashore for a gathering of Eclaireurs Scouts (and Eclaireuses too), on the Naval dock-yard sports ground. At the close, my mother was presented with an enormous bouquet of flowers behind which stood a small and terrified *louveteau* or Wolf-cub. It was always an embarassment to my mother to be given flowers, particularly when she was in uniform, so she had gradually let it be known. The information went fluttering across the world – please no bouquets – please *no* flowers! On this occasion she had the happy thought, it being All Souls' Day, to be taken to the War Memorial where she placed the flowers at the steps; this was considered a very appropriate and tactful move.

No Flowers Please – and also No Autograph Books! When being mobbed by a crowd and having little pages – or even scraps of paper – thrust under one's nose by clamouring signature-seekers, it is virtually impossible to cope with them, and so it was made known that all autograph-hunting was also taboo.

We steamed on through the Suez Canal, Betty and I enjoying our first sniff of the East and fascinated by the 'gulli-gulli' man who climbed up the ship's side on to the deck and kept producing more and more brass cups, corks and handfuls of live baby chicks out of his voluminous white robes.

At Colombo we temporarily parted company with the Waltons, as they sailed straight on to Australia and thence to Tasmania, rejoining us again at Melbourne at the end of the year.

We took another ship to Malaya and landed at

Foxlease, the Guide Training Centre at Lyndhurst

Me and Captain Smith

Helping 'Pickie' hoist the flag

SCOUTS, GUIDES, AND A BROWNIE

'The Barn'

Pax Hill

Drawing-room

'The Barn'

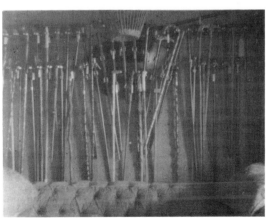

Dad's walking-sticks

Library

PAX HILL

Penang where, despite messages saying 'landing private', groups of enthusiastic Scouts were waving on the quay. This was a fore-taste of our train journey the whole way down the Malayan peninsula, with a few days spent at both Kuala Kangsar and Kuala Lumpur. Wherever the train stopped, there were cheerful, waving brown boys on the platform. What beautiful railway stations they all were – neat and well-kept with white railings and lovely vividly coloured flowers, and with the names of the places written up in English, Malay, Chinese and Tamil. Although the Scouts had been asked not to come on the railway, it didn't stop them; they said they just couldn't help it. It was very tiring for Dad to have to keep turning out to see these boys; luckily however, we had been provided with a special carriage, usually available for provincial residents travelling to visit other states, coupled on the back of the train and he could wave to them from the verandah. At Segamet a crowd of boys, all sorts of races mingling together, came swarming round the carriage. A diminutive Chinese under an enormous topee shouted 'Three cheers for the Chief' and they all joined in, running and waving after the train as it drew gently out of the station.

We were glad to step on board ship again after all those Rallies and official functions and sailed from Penang to Singapore. We secretaries were kept well occupied by our 'employers'; we whispered together in the background at Rallies, trying to discover the names of the hard-working organizers so that we could help write letters of appreciation, congratulation and thanks. We typed out messages for different Scout and Guide groups and for the Press and we helped make up reports on our progress to send back to Headquarters in London.

We had our frivolities too. The typewriters were pushed aside when told that the horses were waiting and we were to be taken out riding through the palm groves – but beware of falling coconuts! We swam in the Kangsar River and sat on banana leaves to whizz down the steep slippery banks of smooth red mud into the water; we were taken out to dinner parties, and at night, under the coloured lanterns, watched graceful Chinese girls dancing in their tight, high-necked silk dresses and split-sided skirts.

It was in Singapore, I think, that the crunch came (it had probably been brewing up throughout the voyage) on the subject of make-up. '*Not* lipstick, darling, you know how Dad hates it,' was Mum's plea to go back upstairs and wipe it all (well, nearly all) off again. We tried to use it as discreetly as possible in the hope that they would not notice. Vain hope! Here, where we were staying at Government House, the Governor's wife and Bridget, their daughter, were so elegantly dressed, so beautifully made up that our plain, gleaming faces and inferiority complexes were getting the better of us.

Mum had never touched a bit of make-up, never heard of mascara (or thought it was a pill) in her life, and therefore deemed it unnecessary for her daughters to do so either. But then, she had no idea of self-adornment in any way; she wore no jewellery (except one pearl necklace with evening dress), no rings, apart from her plain gold wedding ring, – she didn't need any, for her radiant face and smiling expression shone more than a thousand jewels.

But what about we poor plain girls, longing to brighten our lips and lower our long, silken lashes! We argued all together, for and against; those who didn't like it versus those who did; why must *we* be forbidden because *they* disapprove; why can't we do our 'thing' and why don't they wish us to do as our generation do; why must their wishes for us over-ride ours, and so the discussion went on, back and forth. Compromise was eventually reached, with Moderation the key-word. The generation gap would always be there, and we all had to meet each other half way!

Sweet reasonableness now prevailed and apart from this major show-down our parents were really far more discerning, sympathetic and understanding of the ways and aspirations of the young than we realised. Not till the whole tour was over and we flopped into the sofas at Pax once again could we reflect that never a cross word had passed between us!

From Singapore the ship *Marella* (Star of the Sea, the Captain told us) sailed by many Indonesian islands, threading its way by Java and then across the 'shark-infested Timor Sea', touching at Darwin before going on by Wednesday, Thursday and Friday Islands, through the Torres Straits to Townsville and on to Melbourne.

We had three ports of call along the Javanese coast, with attendant Rallies of cheerful Dutch Scouts as well as Javanese, Sumalese and Madurese, at Batavia (later to become Djakarta), Semarung and Sourabaya. Scouting seemed to flourish here, having been introduced from Holland as long ago as 1912, and had really taken a hold with all the right interpretations.

Dad was very anxious to see the ancient Hindu temple of Boroboedoer, which he had heard about when we were in Singapore. Cars were provided and arrangements rapidly made for us to make a quick dash there, straight from the Rally on the new motor-cycle track, before the ship was due to sail again. This ancient temple, all seven tiers of it, in pyramidial form, had lain buried under lava from the nearby volcano, Merapi, and had thus remained preserved for many centuries. When Sir Stamford Raffles, as Governor, came to hear the rumours of its existence, he set 200 coolies to work clearing away the jungle and vegetation and gradually each terrace was brought to light, revealing, all told, seventy-two bell-shaped *dagobas*, each one with a cross-legged Buddha sitting inside. Our arms weren't quite long enough to reach in and touch one of them, as they sat there through the ages, gazing out from their latticed stone bells.

'Australia,' Dad said while drawing us a map, 'is like the head of a lion (pointing west) and a rabbit (pointing east) clamped together like a diphthong.' I thought it looked as though the Rabbit's head was about to eat Tasmania.

We arrived at Melbourne – after spending Christmas Day on board ship – in time for the opening day of a Pan-Pacific Jamboree. This was held at Frankston, where nearly 300 acres of virgin bush was being transformed into a 'canvas city', twenty-six miles out along the sea-coast to Melbourne's holiday resort on Oliver's Hill. On a little knoll was the Lodge, overlooking part of the camp and this lovely comfortable cottage had been lent to us, complete with Lily the cook and Minnie the maid, for the whole fortnight of the Jamboree. Here we could spread our luggage, shake out our travel-creased clothes and strew the papers and letters about the dining-room furniture and floor. We made one room into our 'office' in which to attack a large amount of mail which had accumulated upon the hall table, awaiting our arrival. It included piles of Christmas cards and a long and glowing letter from Peter, enjoying his Rhodesian life and now posted to Umtali.

It was now just under a year since that nightmare day when Dad had been seized with pain and rushed to London for an emergency operation from which it was feared he could not survive. Yet here he was, on the other side of the world, standing out on a dais in the middle of a huge arena, waving his hat in the air to acknowledge the lusty acclamations of a cheering mob of over 11,000 smiling Scouts 'with the same bare knees and ugly faces', as he addressed them, from whatever country they may have come, gathered together to make friends in this brotherly camp city.

The main Headquarters, the nerve centre of the whole camp, run by the State of Victoria, was a wooden building. Then there was the Quartermaster's Store, the Lost Property Office, the hospital (run by the Guides), a shopping centre, the Grandstands at the main arena and three big camp-fire circles. The rest of the camp was then divided into five sub-camps with the different states of Australia acting as hosts in each and each with its own Camp Chief. The Chief Scout visited each of these sub-camps on consecutive days, riding there on a well-trained white police-horse who withstood hundreds of milling, cheering boys with perfect calm and rock-like composure.

On the final day there was a mass Parade of the Wheel of Friendship. The Chief Scout stood on a raised podium at the hub of the great arena with a protective band of stalwart Rovers positioned round the base, and then 'spokes' of Scouts radiated out as a living wheel. From his central rostrum he spoke to them all:

In my own life I have found at least three ways in which difficulties can be successfully met. The first is Duty, the second Fairness and the third, the most potent weapon – Love. . . . A smile and a stick will carry you through most difficulties, but nine times out of ten it is the smile that does the trick. . . . Love is, after all, the spirit of God working within you, like a boomerang, bringing back love from others in return. A man who has no friends is the man who gives out no friendship. A life of love towards others means a life of jolly happiness for yourself – in the words of Mark Twain, 'So live that when you die everyone will feel sorry – even the Undertaker'.

So, Farewell. Go, each one of you from here, as a messenger of Love and Goodwill to others, and Godspeed your effort.

With these words, he then handed out token boomerangs, branded and decorated with kangaroos and kookaburras, which passed from hand to hand and eventually one was presented to each nation which had sent Scouts to the Jamboree.

Following the Jamboree, many contingents of Scouts set off to hike through the bush to Gembrook, the Australian equivalent of Gilwell Park in England, more than fifty miles away from Melbourne. Arranged in small patrols of mixed nationalities (only one from each country in each group) they set forth, with packs on their backs, thumbsticks and the ever-important tea-mug, to trek through the wild forest country of Gippsland, bivouacing or camping at night. The routes, some longer or tougher than others, had all been mapped and pioneered in advance by Rovers from Victoria State during their free week-ends.

Hot, dusty, sun-burnt, some blistered and foot-sore, but all smiling and singing, parties of them were constantly trooping in through the tall gum trees and under the wooden archway of the training-camp. Black boys and brown ones, yellow and white, they trudged in, hailing other Jamboree friends as they converged here. Some of them made straight for the pool, swimming out to the rock in the middle which was swarming with sun-bathing Scouts.

At night-fall, with tents lit in forest clearings, a big camp-fire had been built, pyramid-shaped, in a space of hollow ground surrounded by a circle of logs for seats and a big timber chair for the Chief Scout. As he approached the fire was lit, but apart from the Fire Patrol, there was neither sight nor sound of any other Scouts. At a given signal hundreds of blanket-covered figures came running out of the darkness into the fire-light, emitting blood-curdling yells, then crouched in sudden silence within the circle of light from the flames. Led by Archie, the camp-fire leader, leaping round in a veritable war-dance of conducting, they burst into song – 'Rolling Home', 'The Pirates' Song', 'Down by a Billabong' and of course 'Waltzing Matilda' and the Jamboree Chant. Singing alternated with play-acting, mostly skits on topical incidents from the Jamboree and notably mimicking themselves as foot-sore hikers hobbling into the camp-fire circle.

The smell of the wood-smoke drifted up through the trees and the singing rose into the velvety black night sky. Then, as the embers died down, the Chief Scout was called upon to say a few words to close the Camp-fire:

Brother Scouts, I shall not pass this way again, but I want all of you gathered here to remember this night, and as you go your ways in the world, your job is to spread and keep alive this

Christian, Betty and me

Deck quoits

Dad joins in the Country Dancing

ON THE *DUCHESS OF RICHMOND*

The Kasbah, Tangier

The 'Duchess of Richmond'

The Kasbah, Tangier

Teneriffe

Sierra Leone

Monte Carlo

1929

spirit of Brotherhood, and by so doing to help to bring about Peace and Goodwill on Earth. Good-night and God-speed to you all.

They all rose to their feet for the quietly emotional singing of 'Taps':

Day is done
Gone the sun
From the sea, from the hills, from the sky.
All is well
Safely rest
God is nigh

CHAPTER EIGHT

1935

When the Australian Jamboree drew to a close my father felt buoyant and rejuvenated; he could relax, rub his hands and feel well content, thanking God that he had been able to live to see the peak that Scouting had reached. It was fulfilling all his aims and being interpreted as he had meant it to be – the playwright was pleased with the players.

Although now approaching his seventy-eighth birthday, he walked and talked as a man of fifty; his step light, his voice strong and his stamina completely revived. So much so that when Mr Luxton and two friends suggested that he could justly claim his Scouting 'fee', he went off to Wangaratta with them for a week's fishing on the Kiewa River. He rejoined us at Albury, travelling on the train to Sydney and there followed a blessed three days' rest when we took ship for New Zealand.

Rabbits, brambles and ragwort may have been misguidedly introduced into New Zealand, but fortunately *no snakes*. *No snakes* was the thought that pleased my father most, as he edged his way through tree ferns and thick undergrowth along the banks of the Waikato river, 'stalking' a trout. This visit to New Zealand was primarily to be a holiday although my parents couldn't help seeing Scouts and Guides and attending Rallies and a few official functions as well. Already as the ship docked at dawn in Auckland harbour, surrounded by its volcanic looking mountains, Dad was up on the top deck watching a bevy of Scouts on the quay-side performing a Maori *haka* or welcoming dance – stamping and yelling in rhythm and making hideous faces, trying to make their tongues touch their ears.

'I couldn't have done it better myself,' he shouted, 'and now you'd better be off home for breakfast; I want mine too.' They were able to see him again, however, for a magnificent evening Rally was held on their flood-lit motor-racing circuit surrounded by fir trees on grassy banks.

Next day we hired a car for a month and the Waltons did likewise. With 'dogs-body' Mike Abbott as our sort of patrol leader we went off southwards, with no fixed plan. What a lovely change it made after being kept to a tight schedule for the last few weeks and thinking ahead of the programme we would be facing next month in Canada.

The most important piece of luggage for the time being was not so much the typewriters (although they came too) but the long, narrow box strapped on the front bumper of the de Soto containing the fishing rods. After visiting that phenomenon of Nature, the Waitomo Caves, hung with the myriad stars of glow-worms' lights, we went to Taupo for a week. Here we were lent a bungalow (and Mrs Hewitt to 'do' for us) and went fishing every day (including Sundays when we used a yellow fly called 'the Parson'). In no time at all my father had arranged where he would sleep at the bungalow; he put his bed out on the verandah and in the mornings would call out his slothful daughters – as he'd done in South Africa a few years ago – 'lying in bed like hogs in clover, with the sun scorching your eyes out, come and catch the breakfast!' Trout there were in plenty – huge, lazy ones or fine lively fighting ones – and we lived on them for every meal. Having stupidly professed myself rather good at gutting fish, that then became my sole responsibility.

We explored every geyser of the thermal Wairakei Valley, after passing the portly Maori gate-keeper and being given sticks to go and prod about in the boiling, bubbling mud pools. Then we drove away to the south and stayed with friends at Featherston before facing more official functions in Wellington.

Whilst staying with the Riddifords, a huge amount of mail arrived, for it was my parents' birthday, their joint birthday which in later years came to be celebrated as Thinking Day by Guides and Founders Day by Scouts all over the world. February 22nd was also George Washington's birthday and it was my father, I think, who wrote the little ditty:

George Washington and I
The same birthday were allotted.
Like him, I couldn't tell a lie –
Without it being spotted.

We attended a Thinking Day Service in Wellington, a 'Scouts' Own' open-air Rally and Service at which Gran Walton was invited to read the lesson, 1 Corinthians 13. Betty and I could hardly conceal our giggles when Granville, his great burly figure standing at the lectern, had to read out 'I am as a tinkling cymbal'.

Crossing the Pacific we thought would be a calm and peaceful experience. On the third night out from Wellington, however, we were woken by the constant blaring of a siren and – I will quote from my diary:

At 2 a.m. we were rudely aroused by nearly being tossed out of our bunks. *Maunganui* was rolling heavily, our port-hole was shut and waves kept slapping against it. Peering out, there was only inky darkness and the flash of white waves. Suddenly our hooter started going

– blowing and blowing without pausing for breath. While Betty was enquiring of Dad what all the fuss was about, a seaman in huge boots went past and said that the aerial had fallen down and was pulling the string of the siren.

We climbed into bed again and had to hang on tight to prevent ourselves from being rolled out. We slept at intervals but not very well and when it was light we had an amusing time watching all our luggage come sliding out from under the bunks and go swishing backwards and forwards across the cabin floor. Outside, driving rain and clouds down all round us and grey waves rushing at us in angry great mountains. We were going ahead very, very slowly, climbing up on top of the waves, then bumping down on to them and the whole ship quivered. Every now and then when she gave an extra lurch there was a resounding crash of falling crockery or chairs tumbling about on the deck above us.

Gaily the bugler sounded 'Breakfast' – he played a different tune on each deck and this morning he gave us 'Life on the Ocean Wave'! Dad got up for breakfast, but we stuck to our bunks as being the safest place to avoid crashing to our doom. On deck Dad reported to us that it was very wet and slippery and the sea so mountainous that it repeatedly obscured the horizon. By lunch-time the sea had gone down a bit and the sun was coming out and by late afternoon the storm had abated.

Afterwards it was reported by the Captain that we had 'met and passed through a cyclonic storm, commencing at 1 a.m. and continuing till 3 p.m. At many times the wind reached hurricane force and the seas were terrific.'

Dad had enjoyed every minute of it! He loved a good battering at sea! He had had plenty of nautical experience in 'the little ships' as a boy when acting as crew to his elder brothers. First they had a 5-ton cutter and later on acquired the 10-ton *Koh-i-noor*, with moorings at Shanklin. Whenever they could get together they were off sailing in the Solent or cruising about the south coast and they formed a very competent crew. He never forgot the moment, in extremis one day, when they were caught in a gale off Torquay and he thought, as he hung on grimly, that all was lost. Suddenly there was a booming voice in his ear – furious brother Warington shouting 'Save that boat-hook, blast you!'

One thing that Uncle Warington insisted was that his crew should be able to swim. My father had been amused when at Charterhouse that the only place to swim was in the River Wey which flows past Godalming below the Copse down Racquets Court Hill. But the notice on the bank where there was a good deep pool read 'NO BOY MAY BATHE UNTIL HE CAN SWIM'.

Another excitement of the Pacific voyage was a visit to the South Sea Islands of Raratonga and Tahiti. When we called at Papeete, on Tahiti, we took on board a film company who had been making *The Mutiny on the Bounty*. Frank Lloyd,

'A Frosty Morning', R.B-P.

The Nicest Thing in the Xmas Holidays.

Our Christmas Card

Dad at work

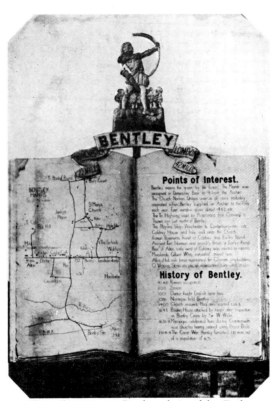

The village sign at Bentley, designed by Dad

Mum at work

HOME

ST. JAMES'S, WEST MALVERN.

TIME TABLE.

No. in Form 8
Average Age 14-11

Form **IV**   Name *Heather Baden Powell.*   Age 14.8   Term *Easter* 1930

	MONDAY.	TUESDAY.	WEDNESDAY.	THURSDAY.	FRIDAY.	SATURDAY.
9. 0.	Painting.	9.9 Drill		Singing.	Science	Painting
9. 55	"	9.40.		German.	German.	"
10. 35	"	10.20. Grammar.	Literature.	Geography.	Scripture.	
11. 15	Aural Training	11. REC	REC.	REC	REC.	REC
12. 0.	Guides.	11.20 French.	Scripture		Arithmetic	French
		12.0 German.	Drawing		Drawing.	
2. 0.	German.	1.50. Games.	1.45.			
2. 40		3.30 "	2.25.			
3. 20.		3.45 TEA	2.45 Game			
4. 10	Change	4.10.	2 Game			
4. 30	TEA	4.50. Composition	Game			
4. 50.	Dancing.	5.30	4.45. TE			
5. 30	"	6.10	5-6. Free			
6. 10	Change	6.50 Hobbies.	6.7 Dra			
6. 30.						
6. 50.						

Swimming

Greek dancing

Me, back right

AND SCHOOL

the director, was a great B-P fan. 'I have met my hero', he told us and he would dearly have liked to have made a film about him and the Scout Movement. But somehow it never came to pass.

'Bump', said Dad; we had now crossed 'the line' and were back in the Northern Hemisphere, 'so you can't go looking for the Southern Cross any more'. Also we had two Wednesdays running: as we crossed 180° longitude (the opposite side of the world to Greenwich), by travelling eastwards we were gaining an extra day.

When we came in through the Golden Gates to San Francisco we were plunged straight into the hurly-burly of American life. Press reporters and photographers swarmed on board and after we'd struggled ashore with passports and alien cards and stumbled over all the luggage in the Customs shed, we were bundled into waiting Cadillacs. Four police outriders on motorbikes escorted us through the town, sounding their sirens and making everyone clear out of the way as we were hurtled along the streets, narrowly missing the 'poached eggs' in the middle, dodging round the wrong side of street-cars and rushing up long, steep hills with tall houses on either side, till we were 'landed' in a vast, palatial hotel overlooking the bay. Here we were confronted with more Press reporters, more mail and a full programme for the two days to be spent in San Francisco before going on by Seattle to Canada. My parents were whirled away to give broadcasts to the whole of America, interviews were given to Press men and women. Dad was a bit sceptical of lady reporters, since giving one of them a long and careful account of the aims and objects of the Scout Movement, and discovering that all she reported in her journal was a description of the clothes he was wearing and the colour of his eyes and hair!

We ourselves were overwhelmed by the hospitality offered to us, with invitations to visit young people in their own homes, to be taken to a Yacht Club dance that night, after the Scout Exposition (but we were out for the count by then) and to go 'horse-back riding' in the morning. . . . After an early dinner, we all climbed back into our uniforms, stepped into the waiting automobiles and, with Police sirens blaring again, we roared along lighted streets, everyone peering out of street-cars at us as we were whirled to a vast auditorium for the Scout Exposition. My diary relates:

The hall was thronged with people, 16,000 of them it was said – up in the gallery and down in the arena – standing room only. Spotlights glared down on us from the roof, a band of sixteen swarthy Scouts lined up ahead of us and with band playing we processed in pairs through the crowd to a large stage and rows of chairs for all the important guests here this evening. Betty and I sat down with a sigh and looked at each other. On the programme we had seen that there were to be ELEVEN speeches . . .

Fortunately they were all very brief, mostly words

of welcome, to which Dad replied, then Mum, and then Gran Walton gave a little speech followed by the band striking up 'Star Spangled Banner' before some presentations were made. American Scouts had not adopted shorts as part of their uniform. Khaki shirts they wore, and nice red scarves, but always with trousers, or even breeches and puttees. Uniforms – no matter where in the world – must constantly change with the times. Waist-lines go high or low; hem-lines rise and fall, with skirts at thigh-top level or swirling in the dust on the floor, and trouser-legs are drain-piped or flared, as the years and the young dictate.

From Seattle the *Princess Charlotte* conveyed us up the coast to Vancouver Island, with glorious views of the Cascade range and the snow-covered Olympic Mountains beyond. Our schedule allowed us two or three quiet days at Victoria before setting out on a long trans-continental journey, homeward bound, across Canada. Early next morning, however, where had Dad disappeared to? He had gone off to the Cowichan River on a whole day's fishing expedition with Mr Lewis Carey! He came back as pleased as Punch, having had, he said, 'plenty of fun without vulgarity' after getting into a steel-head salmon and having a lively time playing it before, like in all good fishermen's tales, it got away.

After many official engagements we left the Island and crossed to Vancouver for a banquet, yet another Rally and a drive at dusk through Chinatown. Waiting for us at Vancouver station was the *Loch Lomond*, a luxurious Pullman coach, normally used by Vice-regals, which had now been lent for our party to make the 3,000 mile journey across Canada. It had rooms for 'The Waltonians', Gran and Joan, as well as the four of us and quarters for Williams, the steward, and Menzies, the chef, and out at the back of the 'car' was the 'observation portion trailing'.

We went on board at night for the start of the journey, and were sorry to miss the lovely scenery up the Fraser Valley. We woke up to find we'd been 'slipped' at Kamloops, and left in a siding. Betty and I found horses awaiting us and we were taken out riding around Kamloops, and then had to dash back to scramble into uniform to go to a Rally in a huge gymnasium (luckily indoors, we'd been so cold out riding). Next day, with two engines pulling us, we climbed up from the Columbia Valley into the Selkirks and on through the Kicking Horse Pass where I wrote 'It is wonderful scenery up here in the Rockies with high snowy mountains towering above us on either side so high that we have to lie down on the floor of the carriage to see the peaks.'

Once over the highest point of the railway at the Great Divide, we entered Alberta and came to rest at Banff. We wanted to see some of the wild animals in the National Park – elk, bison and those yaks with hair hanging down like skirts, but no bears were yet visible, as they were still hibernating through the winter. Betty and I came back to the *Loch Lomond* at dark, but where were our parents? We looked anxiously at the Waltons, but nobody knew where they were and we gazed about us, fears mounting. 'Will you be our guardians,' Betty asked them tremulously, 'in case they never come back?' They had gone out beaver hunting in the dark. Listening hard, they heard a gnawing noise and a crackle of alder brushwood out across the lake. By shining their torch along the water they caught a glimpse of a beaver swimming straight towards them – smooth and brown with whiskers and a rat-like head and long teeth; little ears folded back. It followed the pool of light on the water and came right in towards the shore, with shiny body half out of the water and flat, broad, fleshy tail streaming out behind as he glided silently forwards, blinking at the light of the torch. Then his nerve failed him – he suddenly dived under a bush overhanging the water's edge and was gone.

We had two ports of call in Alberta, the first stop being Calgary, where at night we sped forth in cars out across the prairie to see the flaming chimneys of the oil-fields at Turner Valley. Next day we visited the Sarcee Indian Reserve. Dad was already an honorary member of this particular tribe, his name being Spotted Eagle, and now they wished to make my mother a member too. She had to kneel down on a specially designed mat in front of the Indian Chief while he dubbed her with the name of – well, this was a bit awkward – a female Otter. They couldn't very well dub her as an Otter Bitch, so it was altered to Otter Woman. 'Wotta-woman' Dad exclaimed and we all joined in an Indian dance round them; the easiest way to fall in with the steps was to attempt a sort of hobble, or to go lame on one foot.

Two hundred miles north across unlimited prairie-land we came to Alberta's capital, Edmonton, where we were confronted with another programme of official functions. The Canadian Scout Headquarters had wisely published an advance pamphlet of the kind of programme we might fulfil. *The Visit of the Chiefs* it was called and there followed:

Object: For them to see and be seen by Scouts and Guides and give encouragement to workers.

They would undertake to

a) See the Press in a group
b) Attend official Welcomes
c) Attend Rallies of Scouts and Guides *jointly*
d) Attend Meetings of Scouters and Guiders *separately*

It was also made clear that they would only remain for one hour at rallies, and that the Chief Scout would speak for not more than five minutes. A further request was that there should be:

a) No Guards of Honour at railway stations [thank goodness]
b) No asking for Autographs
c) No presentations of Bouquets or souvenirs

Dad put in one extra plea, however, that he would

much like to see any Canadian veterans from the Boer War. There were so many men who had gone over to South Africa as soldiers and he was always delighted to have a chat with them – and equally they with him. At practically every Rally these men were given a prominent place, proudly wearing their medals; some would wring him so warmly by the hand that it hurt, others greeted him with tears in their eyes. 'Oh, Canada,' we'd learned all the words by now, as we joined in the singing of their national Anthem, 'Oh, Canada, we stand on guard for thee.'

Setting off eastwards again into Saskatchewan we paused for a day in Saskatoon and next morning woke up to find our train standing still in a fog. No, not a fog at all! We had arrived at Regina in a dust-storm. How extremely nasty, thought Betty and I, and we won't be able to go riding here. Very cold, very windy and very dirty and we didn't want at all to step down out of the train. However, while our parents were taken to meet the Press, we renegade secretaries were told that some horses were ready. This seemed to happen to us wherever we stopped! Apparently a picture had been taken of us in Seattle, standing clutching the reins, with large horses' heads looming over our shoulders and this had got into all the papers right across Canada. Riding was a welcome antidote to driving our typewriters and sitting for hours cooped up in the train – but we still didn't think much to going out in a dust-storm in Regina. We needn't have worried. Some 'Mounties' swept us away into their huge indoor riding

school for an hour's equitation on their beautifully schooled horses. We came back exhilarated and only just in time to wriggle into uniform for a huge luncheon party; 200 Scouters and Guiders and officials were assembled and we were led up steps to sit at the high table on a long, narrow platform – 'We've been put on the shelf' Dad whispered aside to us. There were toasts to be drunk, and Dad rose to give a short and light-hearted speech, chiefly congratulatory on the work already done, but also with an undertone of appeal for more leaders:

What the Movement needs today is more young men with sporting blood as leaders; we want men who are half boys themselves – not old gentlemen who are merely interested in improving the morals of the younger generation.

By Indian Head and Elkhorn we travelled on across the prairies; a twenty-minute stop at Brandon, and thence to Winnipeg, 'the gate between east and west' and here Dad repeated his jingle that had helped us with our geography lessons years before:

Winnipeg the middle of
Winnipeg the middle of
Winnipeg the middle of
Cana, Cana DA!

Out of Manitoba, we were borne along into Ontario and to the Great Lakes. Whilst we were in

Toronto we took a day off to visit the Niagara Falls to see 'a lot of water falling over an edge' as Gran Walton described the awe-inspiring spectacle. It also helped him with *his* geography lessons, he said, to remember that the Niagara river falls from E to O, from Lake Erie to Ontario.

From Ottawa it was only a short haul on to Montreal and the last lap of our journey in *Loch Lomond* to Quebec. While Mum and Betty were attending a meeting of the 'Daughters of the Empire' I went for a walk with Dad along the Heights of Abraham whilst he contemplated his meeting with Cardinal Villeneuve that afternoon, concerning the amalgamation of Roman Catholic Scouts. We looked down over the steep cliff to the St Lawrence far below. We saw Wolfe's Path where he came clambering up with his army to attack Quebec, muttering that thing we were taught in our history books; that he would rather have written Gray's Elegy than face the troops of Montcalm. 'What a funny sort of thing for a General to say when going into battle' we soliloquised.

Another version of the Great Divide occurred at Quebec. It was time for the Waltons to go back to England, for Gran to prepare his way and organize the British contingent of Rovers to go to the Swedish Jamboree in July.

Our trans-continental journey continued into the Maritime Provinces. No more Waltons and no more *Loch Lomond* for we'd now been transferred to the Canadian National Railway, with another car attached to the back of the train, the *Bonaventure*. By the time we had fulfilled a few more official engagements, Dad was not so much tired out by this tremendous journey as champing to get away for some more fishing! Newfoundland still lay ahead of us; its salmon rivers should be abounding in fish. W.A. Lawrence once wrote, 'Off the Atlantic coast of Canada lies a British possession – the island of Newfoundland – whose north-westerly peak almost kisses the shores of Labrador and whose south-westerly extremity lies cheek by jowl with the Maritime Provinces.'

In February we had taken ship from Sydney in New South Wales to leave the eastern sea-boards of the Continent of Australia and cross to New Zealand. Now, in early June, we took ship from another Sydney – in Nova Scotia this time – to leave the eastern side of the continent of America and cross to Newfoundland. Not such a long crossing as the Tasman Sea and not such a large ship; the little S.S. *Caribou* took us to Port aux Basques, named after adventurous early pioneer fishermen who came here from the Pyrenees in man's perpetual quest for cod.

All day we ploughed through the grey seas of the Cabot straits, encountering no ice-bergs at this time of year, though in winter-time, with her specially designed hull, the *Caribou* would make her way 'over' the ice, with engines at full speed ahead, forging through the floes coming down on the Arctic currents. We followed Dad out on deck to take a breath of fresh air but were nearly blown in again by the strrong wind as well as by the strong smell of 'agriculture' – a hundred or so head of cattle being mustered on the fore-deck, standing in rows, chewing or mooing or lying in weather-sodden hay, not really caring whither they were being transported.

As in Canada, a private railway car had generously been put at our disposal by the government of Newfoundland. Thus we were comfortably housed while we dawdled our way right across to St John's. There being so few roads in Newfoundland then, the railway was the main artery and chief means of communication and travel, apart from the intermittent coastal services around her indented shores.

One morning we awoke to find ourselves parked in a siding amidst rivers and forests of silver birches and firs, no roads to be seen at all, in fact very little sign of any human habitation; we had come to Robinsons. George Shears came over from his log cabin close by the River Warden's office and helped us set up our rods. 'Dat's a dandy fly for dese fish,' he commented, selecting a 'silver doctor' from Dad's flat tin box and holding it in his teeth while exchanging it for the Jock Scott on my cast. Dad had his beloved 14ft Greenheart and I followed with my 12ft bamboo, down the sandy path to the railway track. Sitting back to back, we bumbled down the line on a 'speeder', there being no other way to reach the Fishells or Barrachois rivers. Dad cautiously asked Charlie, the cheerful speeder driver, what would happen if we met a train coming along. 'Oh, you must jump for it,' said Charlie encouragingly, 'but wait till the last second then the engine carries the

smashed up speeder forward without fragments of it hitting you.'

Although the fishing season normally began in mid-May, it had been a late Spring this year, the rivers were still running very high and the fish not coming up. As we returned empty-handed at the end of the first two days, Dad optimistically said 'Each blank day is one day nearer to catching a salmon.' One thing we certainly discovered was Newfoundland's rich supply of mosquitoes and black flies, and we had to dress ourselves up 'like meat-safes' to save ourselves from being eaten alive. We used Flit, Nujol, Beat It and what Dad called 'Petronella', as well as Absorbine Junior, Carbolic Vaseline and Minards Liniment to try and protect ourselves from the savage biting onslaughts.

It was under the limestone cliff above the Fishells river bridge that Dad caught a salmon; not very big, only a seven-pounder and not a great fighter, but a good shape and he gaffed it safely and unaided. Despite the exhultation, we had a nasty cold journey home on the speeder, with wind and rain blowing in our faces, but returned to find the news had somehow spread on ahead of us. The people from the village of Robinsons, which was hidden from the station, had gathered to congratulate Dad on his catch and next day it was announced in the St John's papers 'Chief Scout catches Salmon'. So his private fishing holiday was disclosed, just as it was time to put on tidier clothes, and our private 'car' was hooked on to the train and we were moved on to Corner

Brook, where the Humber River flows out into a fjord-like arm of the sea. Here we were looked after by people of the international Power and Paper Company and shown all over the paper mills; the life of the whole community was concentrated on the manufacture of newsprint, which was stacked in mountainous heaps. The logs had been floated down the rivers to the mills and the machinery never ceased in its day and night humming, driven by powerful hydro-electric power from the Deer Lake some thirty miles away, pulping and processing the cords of timber hewn from the forests.

Our rail journey across Newfoundland continued eastwards and running parallel with the Exploits River we reached Grand Falls. Many years ago, sitting in their office in London studying a map of the world, the Harmsworth brothers were considering possible resources of newsprint supply to feed the maws of their presses which daily churned out thousands of copies of newspapers to the British public. In Newfoundland they saw possibilities of raw materials, of standing timber and of water power from the fast rivers, and they conceived plans to make use of these natural resources for founding their paper industry. They chose this site of Grand Falls as having all the natural amenities for the manufacture of newsprint, as well as shipment from nearby Botwood.

We were shown all the processes the wood had to pass through from the time the trees had been felled in the forests and become logs to be floated down the rivers. Held in 'holding' booms, they had to wait their turn to go through the barking drums, which Dad called Eton and Harrow because it was a place 'where many were jumbled together and got their rough edges knocked off them and came out trim and orderly'.

Finally we reached St John's and began to feel we were getting nearer home, as we were told it was only 1,933 miles to Liverpool. It was from Cabot Tower, here on Signal Hill, the bluff over the Narrows to the harbour, that Marconi's first successful trans-oceanic test had been made in 1901. We complained that during all the time we'd spent on the island of 'fog, cod and dogs' we'd not yet seen a Newfoundland dog. The situation was quickly remedied and we were taken out to meet some of the champion breed of these creatures. They were huge and black and very slobbery; it was a hot day and they felt the heat as they panted and dribbled and slowly walked away into the shade of some apple trees. One of them weighed 157 lbs, we were informed. 'That's a stone heavier than me,' Dad declared, measuring his stature against this canine version of a Shetland pony.

Retracing our tracks westwards back across the island, it became irresistible to stop at Robinsons again, just for an extra couple of days, to have one more fling at those fish. What a chance in a lifetime it proved for me! Under the guidance of Jack, 'we goes furder up de river' and I landed a 16-pounder after a fearsome ordeal! It screamed away with my line, running out the backing as well. Luckily Jack grabbed the rod from me as I was being towed rapidly downstream, faster than I could move as my heavy old waders were filling with water. Worse than being run away with out hunting, I gulped afterwards – at least one can abandon a horse and someone will catch it – but who's going to catch my fish? Jack floundered away downstream for nearly half a mile before I could get below him on to a sandy reach and could take back my rod and my fish, still fighting; but it was under control now, Jack gaffed it and with his priest, delivered the final blow.

My father's face lighted with pleasure when we rejoined him further downstream and without saying a word, Jack slid the silver monster out of his carrier-sack onto the grass and we stood around in ecstacy, guessing the weight.

So it became time to pack up and leave Newfoundland; drying the lines, folding up the waders, dismantling the rods and reading the poem on the wall of George's hut:

> *Give me a rod and some tackle*
> *To hold fast the thrilling strain*
> *When a fresh run fish is pulling*
> *Like the Century Limited train,*
> *Let me fish 'neath a roaring rapid,*
> *Let my eye just follow the cast*
> *As it dips to the tug from under*
> *When the king of the pool is fast.*

The end of this world tour was nearly in sight and my parents had been given luxurious 'State Cabins' in the *Majestic*, sailing from new York for the final phase of the journey. We had a few days waiting at Boston and even flew a little way. We flew to Washington at the invitation of President Roosevelt, who was President of the Scout Association, to lunch with him at the White House.

On 26th July we tumbled out on to the doorstep of Pax, welcomed by the Wades, Annie, smiling dogs, in fact all the 'Home Office'. And now for a few relaxed days at home. Not at all! The very next day Dad was off to London on the early train and joining Gran Walton once more, went straight away to Sweden for another Jamboree and a Rover's Moot afterwards. Such was the unceasing mobility of this indefatigable 'young' man of seventy-eight!

Returning from Sweden in mid-August there was only an eight-week spell in England before we were boarding ship once again, 'the Parentage' and their secretary-daughters. 'Hither and Thither' we'd overheard ourselves being labelled, but my mother (without having been near a roulette table) thought about us as Rouge et Noir. 'My Children' she found an inadequate definition – 'You could be three or thirty-three with that description,' she complained and she came to the cumbersome conclusion that we were her nearly grown-up daughters. (The jarring term 'teenager' had not yet arrived!)

Now we were bound for Africa.

CHAPTER NINE

1935

As on the previous voyage, the main reason for the exercise was to attend another Jamboree in the Southern Hemisphere and again early in another New Year, 1936. But this journey, too, had delightful detours.

Again we set sail from London docks in mid-October and, as before, the Bay of Biscay was as calm as the proverbial mill-pond. Dad had now crossed here more than forty times – and even I in my tender years had done ten crossings in the last ten years!

So we waved to Cintra, to Cape St Vincent lighthouse and to the obelisk on the sandy cliff of Trafalgar as to old friends. Through the Pillars of Hercules with Gib standing strong and impregnable to port and Tangier, 'all mosques and camels', to the south, we passed into the Mediterranean. Dad spotted a 'huge silver cigar' floating through the air. It was the Graf Zeppelin.

We were rather dreading reaching Marseille. Marshal Lyauty, who had been Chief Scout of France, had died about a year ago, and now they were going to 'transporter à Maroc le corps de notre chef défunt'. They hadn't fixed the date exactly; they were 'keeping' him till we came along, so that Dad could attend the funeral rites and render homage. However, coming into the Gulf of Lyons our ship was caught up in the mistral and delayed, so that we only reached Marseille in time to see the battleship *Foch* coming out of the harbour, covered in wreaths and with tricolour at half-mast on its way to Morocco.

This time when we reached Port Said we were not on duty (although there was a small ambush of Scouts amongst the railway wagons and pontoons on the dockside). We sped away to Cairo for the night, to see the pyramids. We saw them by moonlight and stood with shoulders up close to measure ourselves against the enormous blocks. Each block was more than 5ft high and piled up to a height of 400 feet.

Dad was out on the balcony early next morning as we ran out to see the sun shining yellow on the pyramids, yellow like the sand all around them. We rode camels which were lying down ready for us to mount – Dad's camel made a fierce hissing noise with its mouth wide open until its driver in his long white nightie and red fez told it to shut up. Forward, back, forward, they jerked to their feet and we rode off in single file behind the dragoman on his white donkey, his legs dangling on either side, nearly touching the ground.

Humping up the hill between Khephren and the little pyramid, the camels moving their necks as clucking hens do and their great spongy feet spreading out in the hot sand, we went on out to the right to look at Cheops with its marble-smooth top. Down a sandy track and round the corner of a dune we came upon the huge figure of the Sphynx lying, paws outstretched, in a pit. Last time Dad had seen her she was completely covered by sand except for her head. Now brick walls were being built to stop the encroaching sand.

We caught up the ship again at Suez and she took us slowly through the Red Sea to the east coast of Africa, calling at Port Sudan and Aden. At Port Sudan, by the light of a blazing camp-fire, we watched Hadendowa Scouts acting and clowning, singing and dancing to their rhythmic goat-skin drums, and when Dad was asked to speak to them at the end, he had a horde of interpreters round him who all wanted to show off their mastery of English. Some of the Scouts had come from Khartoum, a 24 hour journey away, and most travelled for miles from inland wastes and had never seen the sea or been in a train before. One of them thought the sea was breathing and alive, and took a bottle to capture a bit of it to take back to show his friends.

Dad had not wasted the day in Port Sudan; he went off deep-sea fishing with the harbour-master all afternoon, and caught a benito. He was reeling it in when suddenly a shark came and seized on to it, so he had a lovely time, he said, pulling in two fish at once! But in the end the shark took away the benito so there was no way of knowing whether or not he was just telling us another fisherman's tale. On his desk at Pax he always had before him that famous prayer:

> *Lord, suffer me to catch a fish*
> *So large that even I*
> *In talking of it afterwards*
> *Shall have no need to lie.*

Towards the end of the voyage to Mombasa there was a Fancy Dress dance – as there was on most ships we'd travelled in. My parents did not partici-pate but they helped us to dress ourselves up. Sister Betty usually became a Chinese coolie – bare-footed and in her pyjamas, her sleek black hair severely brushed back and plaited into a tight little pigtail, she was allowed with a make-up pencil to draw a sloping black line back from her eyes. A kanderstick over her shoulder with little baskets of oranges balanced at each end, and she was ready for the parade along the deck and through the main saloon. My father then helped me to dress up – as himself! Borrowing most of his uniform, including broad-brimmed hat and thumbstick, and caricatured with a fine red nose and false moustache from the barber's shop, I too was ready to join the march. The 'biter bit' was when Bjorn Kuhle, a young Danish lad going out to coffee-farm in Kenya, came and borrowed my Guide uniform to go to the dance – dressed as me.

The first to come on board to greet us on landing at Mombasa were Mrs Wade's brother-in-law, 'Armie', and his wife. He was Sir Armigel, Chief Secretary and Scout Commissioner for Kenya, and they conducted us in a sumptuous white railway coach with gleaming brass railings on the overnight journey up to Nairobi. This was not the first time B-P had visited East Africa; he had joined brother Frank here in 1906, on his way back to England from South Africa, for a big-game shooting trip. Here he was, nearly thirty years later, with an entourage of family, and hundreds of Scouts and Guides waiting to greet him all the way through these territories as he travelled by. Here also was the same bronze statue of Sir William McKinnon, standing in the heart of Mombasa. It still had not moved, although when first erected there, natives had sat down to watch it, to see when the bronze would first move.

Scouts of all colours were gathered on the Kabete showground for a huge Rally; later on, with band playing, there was a garden-party in honour of the B-P's in the grounds of Government House. Hardly were these ceremonies and greetings over than we were climbing back into the Governor's white coach to continue the journey up into Uganda. The engine expired near Kaliro and we were taken on by relief cars and at Jinja had our first glimpse of the vast Lake Victoria, with its abundance of hippos and crocodiles. We were told that the Golf Club at Jinja had a special rule which applied to no other golf course in the world – that a player may lift his ball if it falls into a hippo's footmark.

From Kampala we were driven 24 miles out to Bado to visit what we were told was a Scout Camp. When we got there we could see neither tents nor Scouts, not a sign. On the slopes of a long, grass-covered hill, however, scattered with bushes and palm trees and interspersed with tall ant hills, were some grass-thatched huts, blending into their surroundings. The Scouts, instead of going to all the expense and trouble of buying and transporting tents, had built themselves splendid little huts out of just such materials as they could find around them – reeds, grasses, bamboos, palm leaves, even mud. They built them amazingly quickly, each one large enough to hold about twelve boys, and out at the back they fixed up kitchen shelters with more thatched roofs of reeds and grass.

Out of the surrounding jungle there came a swarm of over a thousand Scouts! A camp fire was lit at sun-down and round it they sang chants and choruses, danced and mimed and played guitars, long into the African night. They acted mock leopard hunts and warriors' scenes carrying spears (stiff grasses) and shields (Scout hats) and, dressed in skirts of palm leaves, they came crouching into the firelight, leapt across the circle and flopped down at the feet of their Chief. As we were all finally making our way back along the paths to the cars, a mass of Scouts came crowding gently after us, stamping rhythmically and chanting 'Menangi, menangi' – my friend, my friend.

'If I have a heaven, this will be mine', explorer Mary Kingsley had said as she dipped herself at the water's edge of an unknown lake in West Africa. This same sensation must have overwhelmed my parents when Eric Walker led them to the spot he had prepared for them beyond the Outspan Hotel, at Nyeri. As a young man Eric had been the Chief Scout's secretary and it was he who had interviewed and captured the then Miss Nugent, now Mrs Wade, to work in the original Scout Office. In the First World War he had joined the Royal Flying Corps and was shot down and taken prisoner at Mainz, from whence he was always trying to escape. Once he slipped out and, by lying up in hiding by day and creeping forward at night, guided by a compass he'd had sent to him hidden in a pear, he eventually reached a canal at the Dutch frontier. With great relief, having been at large for five weeks, he gave himself over to the sentry. But then, oh horror! It was a German sentry! There were two canals running parallel, and he'd only swum the first one.

When he eventually returned to England after three-and-a-half years of imprisonment, he couldn't settle down to anything and for some time led an exciting, roving life (and wrote a book without revealing his real name) rum-running in America, in those days of prohibition. Tall, gay, with roguish blue eyes and an ever adventurous spirit, Eric then found Bettie, daughter of Lord Denbigh. He proposed to her, he said, sitting out at a 'deb.' dance, on the back stairs of a smart London house. When they were married, they stood on the edge of England and said to each other, 'Which way shall we go from here?' Should it be westwards and try silver-fox farming in Nova Scotia, or eastwards to Kenya and try coffee-farming? They decided on the latter and off they went to look for a plot of land in the highlands of Kenya. On arriving at Nyeri they had a very rough time and found extremely poor accommodation. It was then that they decided what Kenya needed most was better hotels. They wrote home to Bettie's father, telling him their views and ideas and received a cable back – 'Good luck to the Denbigh Arms'. So, without hesitation they set to work at Nyeri and made the idyllic hotel, with the more appropriate name for a halting-place in Africa, The Outspan, facing across the forty mile wide valley to the ever-changing view of Mount Kenya.

For many years Eric and Bettie had been trying to persuade my parents to visit them and at last the time had come. This truly was a Heaven upon earth! A bungalow with huge verandah, set in a garden ablaze with cannas, red and yellow, and 'pig' or arum lilies, and beyond these the avenues lined by gum trees and showers of blue jacarandas.

Here we had a fortnight in hand before going on down the east coast of Africa in time for the Jamboree at East London at the end of the year, and so here our caravan rested.

Out came the fishing rods, for here were the

Amboni and Thega rivers well stocked with trout, waiting to be fished (at one spot a notice to fishermen said BEWARE OF RHINOS). Besides this, my father wanted to find some big-game shooting. Not shooting to kill, but shooting with a cine camera, to have film to keep and to see, over and over again. He had shot big game in the past, the walls of the barn at Pax were surrounded with trophy heads and horns; eland, impala and scimitar-like sable; oryx, kongoni and cork-screw horned kudu, and the fierce, flat horizontal horns of the buffalo; skins of zebra and lion and heads of wild boar with their nasty upturned tusks.

'I never want to shoot another elephant,' Dad had once stated, 'it causes such a BIG death.' Just a few years previously he had been presented with a 'black box' by Mr Eastman. George Eastman, head of the big Kodak Company in America, had two great ambitions; one was to improve the looks of American men, which he set about doing by promoting a greater use of false teeth; the second was to try and bring about peace between nations. He thought my father had done so much towards this end that he presented him with two cine cameras, a projector and several 100 ft reels of 16mm film, in recognition of the work of the Scout Movement.

Armed with this 'shooting' apparatus, Eric led us away on safari, to look for game. Pip Beverly, a young farmer and white hunter, went on ahead with a lorry-load of tents, supplies and native 'boys' to make camp at the Kipsing River, away in the northern part of Kenya, beyond Isiolo. We followed with Eric by car and came in at dusk to find a magnificent camp set out in the wilds amongst thorn-trees and scrub – and a three-course meal served to us in a dining shelter. 'Is this living rough, in Darkest Africa?' we thought. Darkness fell very quickly and a huge fire was lit and kept burning all night to keep the wild animals away and we hung our lanterns outside our tents for the same purpose. We could hear the noises of hippo wallowing in the river, of monkeys barking in the tall trees by the water and hyaenas yowling quite close by our camp as they trotted to and fro.

Dad, the early riser, was always one of the first to be up and about the camp, and we came tumbling out at half light, to be off in search of game. Standing by the dying embers, leaning on his spear, was a gigantic figure, very tall, very black, a Turkhana tracker; very supercilious too, but he could quickly change his expression and become a complete buffoon, imitating himself tracking down game. With him he had one whom my father called 'The Plumber's Mate', a hideous fellow with terrible teeth and a large safety-pin in his red mud-matted hair. Turkhanas hunt in pairs, and will never go into the bush after game alone.

These two led us forth at dawn, with Pip and Eric carrying loaded rifles, tracking the animals that had been prowling around in the night. There were the huge round prints of hippo and in the sand we found spoor of all different sizes of buck as well as the dog-like paw-marks of hyaena and the tiny slots of dikdiks. Amongst the bushes we

68

saw zebra, Grant gazelle and a lovely grey oryx with very long horns, loping away to take cover.

We returned to camp for the heat of the day, lying in the shade as the animals all do, and then went prowling again in the evening. But to try and get shots with the camera we had to set out at first light each day, coming back into camp for breakfast.

Pip had been reconnoitring even further afield to see if he could find lion. He came upon a camp of Somali tribesmen who had just had a donkey stolen by a lion, who had dragged it off to some rocks about a mile away. By the time we reached the place they indicated, there was not a sign – only some lizards scurrying over the rocks and two foxes who went lolopping off into the long grass, and some marks in the sand where a rhino had been lying down, leaving little corrugations imprinted by the pattern of his hide.

As in Uganda, there were huge anthills of red sand dotted amongst the thorn bushes, some more than six feet high. Not all were inhabited by ants; we saw several occupied by kitate – funny little brown animals my father described as 'a cross between a squirrel and a gopher'. They scurried across the road and hurled themselves by flying leaps into their burrows, by one of the many entrances.

On the road back to Isiolo we encountered a vast community of storks – 'black-coated old gentlemen standing bent with their hands behind their back' was the way Dad described the maribou. There were hundreds, all wandering about or standing with their wings stretched out, drying in the sun. As we approached they flapped along the ground then lifted themselves heavily into the air, their ugly great long legs hanging clumsily behind them. Overhead were millions more of them, flying round and round and circling a long way up into the sky.

Soon after passing back through the police post, Eric suddenly said 'Twiga' as he sighted a bunch of giraffe, with heads bent over thorn bushes, feeding. We made towards them and they stood their ground for a bit, staring at us from their exalted height and swinging their long tails. There were eleven of them in the group including two totos, or babies. One of them started to move away, and then they all did. They stopped to have a look round in an enquiring way and then bunched together before cantering off. We gave chase for a while but although they appeared to be cantering in slow motion, we couldn't keep abreast of them in the car over the rough ground, and so had to give them best. However, Dad had been able to take some lovely shots before they left us in the lurch, and we returned to human habitation at Nyeri.

'Lynx' Soltau, the pilot whom we had met previously at Kampala where they were formulating plans for airway routes over Africa, helped us complete the next stage of our journey, which was to fly southwards from Kenya. We were flown to Dar-es-Salaam in a six-seater 'Dragon' with two Gipsy engines which could just manage an average speed of 110 m.p.h., but had to refuel at Nairobi

before we set out on the 500-mile 'hop' to Dar. Dad had not often flown before – none of us had for that matter – but it was an experience he greatly enjoyed, particularly looking down and watching vast herds of game grazing on the Serengetti plains. My parents, however, had quite resolved by this time that Nyeri was the place for them, and they left Eric making plans for the day when they would return to the Outspan.

At Dar we boarded a white steam launch for the four-hour crossing to Zanzibar. Scouts and Guides crowded down to the water's edge to see us off, balancing on all available rocks. Waving and singing, they made a colourful sight in their bright uniforms with the brilliantly red flamboyant trees along the shore behind them. Dad discovered that we were accompanying much wealth, as this trip coincided with that of the Treasurer of Zanzibar, bringing in the first new East African currency to replace the then Indian rupees and annas.

When my father had visited Zanzibar in 1906 he couldn't resist taking a railway ticket – because of such a name – to Bu-bu-bu. We couldn't resist it either, although one could easily go there by car now, as it is only a seven-mile journey – seven miles almost entirely composed of clove groves, Zanzibar being 'the Isle of Cloves'. We were taken into warehouses filled to the roof with cloves. 'Whoever could want so many cloves?' Dad asked; 'We only put them in bread sauce and apple puddings, and even then they get in the way!'

The Rally that we were to attend here was held at 9 o'clock in the morning, before the heat of the day, out on the golf course. Some of the Scouts and Cubs performed jungle plays and native dances, while others built huts, plaiting palm leaves together to make the walls and flooring. One boy, with his feet roped together, climbed up a nearby palm tree to show us how they gathered coconuts.

We took ship again from Zanzibar southwards, hugging the edge of the Indian Ocean, bound for Beira. Suddenly, at about 4 a.m., Dad came and roused us when he felt the ship had changed her course, and then she went still. 'Can't have got to Beira already,' we thought, 'we're not due in there for another twelve hours.'

We had been tossing about in a fair old storm and the Captain had stood her further out to sea for fear of getting blown too near inshore. The 2nd Officer had seen a flare but could not make out what it was until he saw another go up – then realised it was from a lifeboat in distress. A German tug towing a lighter of sugar up the coast had taken a list in the heavy seas. The bo'sun had managed to free a life-boat before she turned turtle and sank, and they had been tossing about in the storm-lashed sea for eighteen hours.

We hove to, and soon there came out of the darkness, rising and falling on the huge waves, this little white boat, overcrowded with a huddle of men, desperately rowing towards us. Sometimes it came dashing headlong towards our ship on the crest of a wave – next moment it was lost to view, engulfed in a trough. At last it came alongside only to capsize as the native crew rushed for the pilot-ladder. Arc lights shone down on them from our decks and a whole fleet of life-bouys were thrown overboard. It was not until the last of the crew had been pulled up to safety that the four German officers attempted to get on the ladder, so exhausted by now that they had to be rope-hauled up the ship's side to gain the deck. There they all stood, dripping and miserable and examining one another's cuts and bruises. The Captain made them all sit in a row on the hatch while rum was given them and they were rolled up in blankets and taken below. The poor valiant little life-boat (which Dad badly wanted to 'save' and present to a Sea-Scout group in South Africa) was left floating away into the darkness.

This wasn't the only trouble we ran into on this little voyage. Malaria struck! First Mum was laid low and ran a high temperature, and a couple of days later Dad fell victim too. We could never remember my mother being ill, it was something which never occurred! She was never sick or sorry for herself, had no aches or pains and with the broadest of grins could always truthfully say 'And I've got all me own teeth!'

We were therefore feeling a bit down in the mouth, the weather was still horribly rough and we were having rather a gloomy Christmas – with just a few miserable streamers across the dining saloon – on board ship again, just as we had been this time last year when nearing the Jamboree in Australia.

However, we had one delightful surprise as our ship tied up to a bouy opposite a landing pier at Beira, for coming out on a launch amongst a deputation of Scouters was Peter. He'd managed to take forty-eight hours' leave to come to the coast from Umtali to say Happy Christmas to us, and stay a night on board. We quickly took him to poor Mum's cabin where she was feverishly tossing and turning and mumbling that she felt 'just like a chewed rag'. She cheered up to see policeman Peter and by the time we reached Durban she was beginning to feel better.

By this time, however, it was Dad's turn to succumb and when we reached Delagoa Bay (Lourenço Marques) Betty and I had to 'hold the fort' on our own. We were woken early by the Purser telling us that some Portuguese Scout Officials had come on board and would we please mind sending all the Scouts and Guides off the quay as they were in danger of being slain by the cranes trying to unload the ship! We leapt out of our bunks and into uniform, and found a very sympathetic lot of Scouters, to whom we explained in our best sign-language kind of Portuguese about our Parentage and how they must have been bitten by malaria-laden mosquitoes whilst we were on safari in Kenya.

We called the doctor at Durban, who took blood slides which proved positive the malarial infection; he prescribed Aspirins and Atebrins; and Dad loved it when I held a sponge-bag full of ice against his hot forehead.

CHAPTER TEN

1936

As the New Year of 1936 came upon us, so we came into Buffalo Harbour and landed at East London. My mother was quickly shaking off the effects of her bout of malaria but Dad was not really fit enough to be up and doing. So we smuggled him ashore (the busy little secretaries having wired ahead that there should be no official welcome) and put him straight to bed at the hotel overlooking the sea.

We had a few days in hand before the opening of the Jamboree; we also had the relief and joy of falling into the arms of the Waltons once again, as they had come round by the mail-boat from England to join us here. They felt, as our parents had done ten years previously, that they didn't wish to be separated from their small children while they went to South Africa for six months, so they'd brought two of their three sons with them, also niece Pauline, and Joyce to look after the little boys.

The hotel was at bursting point. Among other celebrities, Jean-Pierre Wimille, Pat Fairfield, Earl Howe and Eileen Ellison, motor-racing drivers all, were still here after competing in the South African Grand Prix on the eleven-mile circuit in the sand-hills the previous week; and next week the Australian cricket team was arriving. We felt at the hub of the universe!

Solomon's Garage had put a car at our disposal and so Betty and I hurried off to the Post Office to enquire about driving licences. 'Oh,' we were told, 'we don't issue them here; you must go to the Revenue Office for them – you know, just opposite the station.' On we went to the Revenue Office just opposite the station. 'You must go to the counter marked "Traders' Licences",' they said, 'we don't issue them here.' Off we trotted again and this time were told, 'Oh, you will have to go to the Fire Station to get the appropriate forms and then go to Captain Burnett to take a driving test'. So away we went to the Fire Station, which we discovered was in Fleet Street, and eventually found ourselves in front of the genial figure of Captain Burnett. Captain Burnett had previously been in the South African Constabulary. He shook us warmly by the hands, smiled benignly upon us and took us out on a short driving test, sending us scurrying home clutching our driving licences (but the poorer by £2 each), which we discovered were valid for the rest of our lives.

Now that we had the car and could legally drive him about, we took Dad out for drives each day, along the coast or round the twisty Grand Prix course (slowly) and even explored surreptitiously up to the entrance to the Jamboree site, with its symbolic Springbok framed in the wooden archway. He enjoyed being driven about and said the psychological effect of being up and about and seeing around him made him feel much better.

My mother was restored to her former energetic self but with the reunion of the 'O.P.', a serious discussion took place. It was decided that this tour, which had already been planned for the next six months, must be curtailed. Gran Walton was horrified by the programme and though he could take a great deal of the load off B-P's shoulders, it was agreed, backed up with a doctor's advice, that the strenuous itinerary we'd drawn up must be drastically trimmed. Instead of touring all through South Africa and Rhodesia until June, we should cut the time and allow Dad a complete holiday, only attending the two major events: the Jamboree now and the meeting of the South African Scout Council in February, six weeks later.

The Jamboree was held on some open land facing the sea, above East London, by the road to Transkei; a national gathering of about 3,000 Scouts from all over South Africa, the Rhodesias and Portuguese East Africa (Mozambique). The City of East London had invited the Scout Council to hold the Jamboree here – offering the site with water, electricity and all amenities laid on. They had even laid on feeding arrangements and kitchens, and had already pitched some bell tents (in serried rows) for those coming without their own equipment. It was a magnificent gesture.

The Camp opened with a flourish; bands playing. Scouts had been arriving 'by the ton'; special train-loads came steaming into the station, some came in lorries and some even by air. In fact any means of transport had been used and many were the interesting tales of long treks with bicycles, ox-wagons and even on Shanks' pony.

The Chief Scout was well enough to stand up on the dais in the middle of the arena for well over an hour, to greet this multitude of Scouts. He spoke to them, loud and clear, and his speech was relayed throughout South Africa. He impressed upon them that they were all gathered here to *be* friends and to *make* friends and let Fraternization and Brotherhood to be key-words in the whole of their outlook.

You fellows will, within the next few years, be the men of the country, and I want to urge you all to make friends now among yourselves so that you will still be friends when you grow up and thus make a united team of good men for South Africa.

The Scouters' Conference was yet to come, but meantime the Guiders' Conference was taking place at one of the Training Centres (or Universities of today) at Grahamstown. My mother, with Betty in tow, went off there while Dad and I remained quietly at East London, resting on a sunny verandah, regaining his health. We were lucky in being able to have the services of a top doctor, Doctor Bruce-Bays, who was also the Mayor of East London. As the Mayor of East London he had invited Dad to a City Reception, and as Doctor Bruce-Bays he had forbidden him to attend!

For me there was one frightening occasion when I prevailed upon him and rang him up in the middle of the night. Dad was seized with a non-stop attack of hiccoughs. 'Go to the chemist', the doctor said, 'and fetch some Sal Volatile.' Out into the dark streets I drove, found the chemist, got a bottle of Sal Volatile, administered but one teaspoonful to my 'patient' and all was well again.

The doctor came daily, and daily Dad and I went off for little strolls or sat on a sunny bench; we drove out to Marina Glen, to the breakwater, or to Naloon to watch the seals being fed, and then back into the town to change books at the Library. One evening we even went to the cinema – he was a great enthusiast for a good film – and saw Ralph Lynn, Tom Walls and of course, 'indubitably', Robertson Hare, in *Stormy Weather*.

Going to the window on the morning of 21st January, the Union flag was drooping sadly from half-mast out in front of the hotel. We knew what it meant; King George V had died. Everything seemed plunged into a state of gloom, even so far from the homeland, and services were being arranged everywhere. Next day came the news that the Prince of Wales had accepted the throne and was being proclaimed King Edward VIII from the steps of the Royal Exchange.

With all the rest of the 'O.P.' scattered about in South Africa, attending Scout and Guide functions and meetings, Dad and I quietly took ship up the coast to Durban to rejoin them there. There we came under the wing of another excellent doctor, Dr Pearson. By this time Dad was passed fit, and was able to attend the Scouters' Conference in the City Hall. They were debating the colour problems of Scouting in South Africa, which was now running in four groups with a central office in Johannesburg to hold them all together.

Also going on at this time were celebrations for my parents' joint birthday 'Thinking Day' ceremony, involving plenty of work for us secretaries, answering innumerable greetings. Dad helped us out by drawing a happy Zulu, in full regalia, waving 'Thankyou' in three different languages – English, Afrikaans and Zulu – and we quickly had cards printed. My father had now entered upon his eightieth year – my mother thirty-two years behind him.

One thing that Dr Pearson 'prescribed' was a visit to the Kruger National Park, where he had recently been himself and brought back some superb film of big game, including lion. This whetted Dad's appetite!

With the conclusion of the all-important Scout Conference – and Dad had not missed a single session – the Waltons boarded ship for England with their family. Mum and Betty went with them as far as Cape Town and then started a working journey through Cape Province from there. Dad and I, left on our own again, dallied a few more days in Durban while we planned a fishing trip.

'Let's have a look at Dick King,' he said one morning as we were walking along the sea-front. Sketch-book in hand, he made a quick drawing of this equestrian statue – a tired man on a tired horse – and then wrote a brief story of this epic ride which we sent back to Mrs Wade in England to publish as one of his 'yarns' in the weekly publication, *The Scout*. He related how a Zulu chief had ceded Natal to the British but when he died in 1842 his successor calmly gave it to the Boers instead. Some British left in Durban were besieged by the Boers and one of them, Dick King, bravely rode forth from the beleaguered town to fetch help. The nearest British garrison was at Grahamstown, 600 miles away, and he rode the distance in ten days, to raise the alarm.

My father was always observant – and also critical – of equestrian statues. His favourite was the Cavalry Memorial in Hyde Park and he chose this as the motif on the cover when he started the *Cavalry Journal*, buff-coloured with the statue impressed in red. This statue vividly portrayed St George and Dragon, he declared, with a proper horse, with muscles and veins depicted in finest detail. The Foch Memorial by Victoria station he liked for the relaxed posture both of the General and of his charger, with its neck outstretched, reins loose. But the futuristic lines of the Haig statue brought forth much expostulation – 'That's no horse,' he said. 'That's a swan.'

In old clothes and with fishing rods, we drove away from Durban up to Pietermaritzburg. Years ago, Dad remembered, his peppery old Colonel, Sir Baker Russell, with mixed metaphors and muddled Malapropisms, had always called this town 'Mary St Petersburg', and when asked how far it was from Durban he'd said, 'Well, as the cock crows, it's about fifty miles'. But taking the road through the Valley of a Thousand Hills as we were now about to do, it's nearer sixty. We drove on for a further sixty miles, to Nottingham Road, deep in the Drakensbergs, to fish on the lovely Mooi River.

My father had fished here last time we were in South Africa, while we children were at school on the Cape. He knew his way to the Avon Waters, the Bend and to Silverdale Farm where he had been invited to fish. Little dark *Umfaans* with outsized khaki shorts came running down the hillside, where they were guarding the cattle, to open the fences across the road for us and we paid them with sugar-stick sweets which set them dancing with delight. With his great love and understanding of children, my father was enchanted by their expressive faces and clapping hands.

After this week's fishing in Natal, Dad was

feeling remarkably fit and well and was right back on his feet again. We'd only had one untoward incident, when I'd managed to drive the car into an ant-bear hole, coming away from the river at dusk. Dad set off towards the nearest farm to find help and came upon a Zulu who immediately knew what was required, and brought along a pair of oxen. A rattle of chains and one good heave on their yoke, and the car was mobile again.

Although we had now cancelled the arduous tour of South Africa, the doctors passed him fit enough to continue his journey up to the Rhodesias, but *not* to penetrate further north than the Victoria Falls for fear of running the risk of meeting another malaria-bearing mosquito! We rejoined Mum and Betty and had a few days together marvelling at the splendour of the falls. We liked the notice on the railway-station which said 'Bicycling on the platform is prohibited'; we walked in the rain forest where the spray keeps the vegetation perpetually watered. The rainbows were fascinating, particularly the upside-down ones – perfect arcs from the depths of the gorge, up through the spray and over the top of the falls. The noise of the roaring waters, pulsing and throbbing, drummed continually in our ears. At night we went out by moonlight to see the Lunar Rainbow, the sight of which made a lasting impression on us all. In my father's words:

. . . Now I know that only those who have communed with the falls by night have really grasped their inward message. In the soft light of the South African moon at the full, I stood and gazed at the stupendous scene.

I doubt if any written words could truly describe the awesome majesty of that immense, dimly-seen procession of water thundering into the depths of the chasm, where it is lost to view, hidden in a dense fog of spray.

Before one, rising into the sky, is a wide semi-circular arch of silvery lunar rainbow. Above it the dark sky is spangled with bright stars; within and framed by it stands, in contrast, a vast luminous film of mist having the light of the moon reflected through it with magic effect from the face of the falling form.

This fairy scene, while it appeals to the eye in its beauty, has as its accompaniment the impressive sound of the thudding roar of the tons of falling waters – a rhythmic diapason which is not of today, or of yesterday, but has maintained its continuous cadence without a stop for tens of thousands of years.

One could only gaze spellbound at the majesty, might and power of it all, as a wondrous manifestation of the work of the Creator, and with a sense of awe such as no ceremonial service, however impressive, in a man-made cathedral could ever evoke.'

(African Adventures)

From a point about a mile further upstream, a launch took us out to Palm Island, so-named because of the palm trees growing there bearing

the hard white fruit called Palm Ivory, which is not quite hard enough to be mistaken for the genuine ivory of an elephant's tusk.

A night's journey took us bumbling away southwards to Bulawayo with a wait there for the connection for a further day's train journey up to Salisbury.

From Lincolnshire to Lancashire
To fetch a pocket handkercher'

Dad repeated in rhythm with the train as we rumbled along across the African veldt, and when we clattered across other tracks he changed the beat to

The Duchess of Edinburgh
Couldn't touch bread-and-butter

repeated rapidly, in a tangle of rolling R's.

Clapping and cheering from a vast crowd of Scouts and Guides greeted our parents as they stepped down on to the platform, and we followed, sleepy and travel-stained, behind them. Waited upon hand and foot, we all stayed at the lovely white Government House, single-storeyed with Dutch style architecture of graceful gables, portico pillars and red-tiled roof. Clusters of orange-yellow creeper covered the walls, and wide verandahs or *stoeps* ran right the way round a central quadrangle of lawn and palm trees. On guard by the flagstaff at the front of the house were men from the B.S.A. Police and what could

have delighted Dad's heart more next morning than being woken by the sound of the old cavalry bugle calls from their barracks.

He had reminiscent little verses which he sang to the different calls as we heard them throughout the day. For the 'Fall In' he sang:

Damn you all, blast you all,
Can't you hear the Bugle call

and for 'Stables'

Get to your Horses and give them some Corn
Get to your Horses and give them some Corn

and then at feeding time,

Feed your horses,
Feed your horses,
Feed the beggars, feed

The next evening in Salisbury we were all led out to a Scout camp-fire, escorted on either side by Rovers carrying flaming torches, and as we halted at the edge of the circle, one of them recited the following welcome:

Amid the grandeur of the massive hills
Amid the silence of the lazy veldt
Amongst the white and hardened granite rocks
Where thoughts of hate and envy quickly melt
Was planted in the mind of young B-P
The seed which sprang into the Scouting Tree.

We welcome now our Chief who stil to us
Imparts his knightly spirit long to live
Around the camp-fire 'neath a starry sky
Our love and loyalty we gladly give
A fleeting visit he is pleased to make
To the land of Rhodes where thoughts of Scouts took
  shape.

The Guides, called Wayfarers, and the little Brownies, called Sunbeams, came and held a Rally in the grounds of Government House to see my mother. As so often happens at this time of year, before sundown there was a sudden deluge. My father was renowned for bringing bad weather to Jamborees and Rallies; he said he did it on purpose, testing out the stamina of Scouts and seeing how they faced up to difficulties – they weren't going to be just fine-weather boys. Now my mother was trying it out on the girls! They crowded in off the gravel, almost ankle-deep in wet, up on to the stoep while the rain tipped down. They sang lovely, rather melancholy songs, but so cheerfully and enthusiastically. The harder it rained, the louder they sang. Their departure was quite dramatic. They were transported away in long mule-waggons, all bundled in and huddled under groundsheets waving and cheering as the six-mule teams galloped away down the drive – a team of all-white mules being particularly spectacular in a sort of chariot-race to the gates.

The next day was a memorable family occasion for us. Peter, stationed as a Trooper in the B.S.A.

Police at Rusapi, had come up here on leave to join us for the last few days of this tour in Africa. His force was now being mechanized, going over to motorbikes instead of horses. Instead of narrow withers in front of him, he mourned, and a nice pair of pricked ears, it would be a shiny petrol-tank and silver handlebars!

The other feature of this day, 16th April, was that it was Betty's nineteenth birthday. Hardly in her wildest dreams could she have believed she'd be back again in Rhodesia within six months – with a husband who shared the same birthday.

The entire B-P family were poured into a special car on the train back to Bulawayo. There were pauses to see groups of Scouts and Guides, cheerfully gathering themselves along the platforms to wave as we passed through Gatooma, Que-que and Gwelo and trundled on our way south.

From Bulawayo we snatched a few hours to drive out to those ridiculous shaped hills, the Matopos. Rather like the trolls in Norway, some laughing giants must have piled up those lumps of rock and scattered them about in the bush. We went in through the gates to Matopo Park, following the road amongst high masses of boulders and monoliths – big slabs of rock with little boulders perilously perched on them.

'I had to find my hill; I had to find it,' Cecil Rhodes had declared and in 1902 he was buried there, a grave hewn in the granite rock on World's View, a kopje in the Matopo Hills.

One thing that Dad said he must do while he

had us all together was to take us for a walk – in Mafeking. So, away to the south we journeyed far! Into Bechuanaland, into Mafeking, all five of us. We could hardly believe where we were, having had the name imprinted, somewhere in our minds, all our lives. 'Mafeking', said a pretty young girl sitting next to Dad at a dinner party once, 'Mafeking! Is that a kind of margarine?'

A funny little place we thought it, with bumpy roads and sad little shops, and yet it should feel full of self-importance, being the administrative town for this Protectorate. We walked by Dixon's Hotel in the market square and saw the bell which was rung whenever a Boer shell was coming; past Crew's Hotel where the shells invariably landed, and then on to the convent, still standing the same as it was during the Siege, but 'it got fairly knocked about then'. He showed us the hospital – the Victoria Hospital – which used to have a big trench leading to it from the middle of the town, so that the wounded could be carried along in safety – more or less. In the market square he showed us the place where he had made his Headquarters and also where he used to sleep. He had his bed out in the open, in front of Dixon's Hotel, with two enormous sand-boxes on either side of him 'for stray bullets to bury their noses in'.

Whenever the bell rang warning that another shell was coming over, everybody had to run for cover in the dug-outs. All the dogs in the vicinity got to know what the bell meant and dashed to get themselves down to safety before the people.

He regaled us with one or two lurid stories too. One indolent fellow, who didn't think he need hurry down into the dug-out when the bell rang, was caught by a shell while sauntering on his way and 'blown to blazes'. Another young man was standing at the bar in Crew's Hotel when he had his head blown off by a ricocheting shell. 'Please, no more!' the female element of our family cried.

Cannon Kopje, the only piece of rising ground in this flat, flat plain, had quite changed its features from the place Dad remembered thirty-six years ago; the bush had all grown up so tremendously and although we tried to find the fort at Game Tree Hill, where they had had some skirmishes with the Boers, so many new young saplings had sprung up that the original tree was lost in the forest.

Finally he took us along to the cemetery where we saw the graves of many soldiers and 'town guards' as the civilians were called. There were, I described, 'a terrible lot of them', and Dad could remember practically every one of them individually, including one in particular called Webb – 'bravest of the brave' he said, in a far-away voice.

We had a few official obligations while we were all there too; the Sisters of the Convent wanted to have a look at us; the Pathfinders and Wayfarers were waiting – as usual, in the rain! – at the Native stadt to give us a welcome and they sang that lovely melodious 'Sikalele', their African anthem which we never grew tired of hearing.

Doctor's orders to my father had been to go and look for lion in the Kruger National Park, in

Rolls-Royces at Pax

Camping, with 'Eccles'

Dad in his fishing clothes

DADDY PUT
FISHING   May 1922

R.B-P.

CAMPING, FISHING, TENNIS

H Baden-Powell.

Peter on Nigger, Betty on Gipsy Moth, me on Starlight, 1933

Painting, 1932

Heather Baden-Powell.

_____ AND MY HORSES _____

eastern Transvaal. Doctor Pearson had lent us an extra cine camera with tele-photo lens and thus well-armed we made off to Nelspruit for a final look for game before taking ship for England.

Colonel Stevenson Hamilton, the Warden, took us towards the rest-camp at Pretorious Kop and by now we were so bouyed up to see lion that we kept imagining we could see one in every tuft of tawny, waving grass. A wildebeeste stood staring at us, poised beside an ant-heap, quite unperturbed, swishing his long, horse-like tail, and further on a bunch of them galloped across the road ahead of us, then wheeled round and stopped to look, or called to one another with a shrill neigh – the Gneighing Gnus, Betty called them. Black stripes on their front ends and shaggy manes and beards and such accentuated Roman noses!

'Lions love wildebeeste to eat,' I wrote in my diary, 'they like them almost more than they do zebra.'

Then we saw some zebra, fat ones, tightly sewn into their stripy suits, trotting away behind some bushes. They suddenly broke into a stiff-legged canter and from out of the bushes behind them trotted a slinking, tawny form. 'It's a lion, it's a *lion*.' We bobbed up and down with excitement – not allowed to move out of the car of course, and engine kept running. A lion sighted at last, then *two* lions; they trotted along quite quietly with the terrified herd of zebra now galloping away before them. Three lions now! We could see them clearly through field-glasses, moving stealthily along the side of the hill. We travelled slowly along the dusty road, keeping parallel with them as they gradually made their way along the ridge. Then we saw they'd stopped and were lying down near the bottom of the ridge where there was a watercourse and tall, thick reeds and bushes. As we drew a bit nearer we could see that they had joined several more lions, all lying down, tearing at the flesh of a zebra and crunching up the bones. Jackals appeared from nowhere, trotting anxiously back and forth, watching the lions feasting and hoping to dart in and snatch a bit for themselves. The terrified zebra were standing at a respectful distance, barking at the loss of one of their herd and trying to keep the lions in sight all the time, so as not to be caught by surprise.

We sat motionless in the car, the only noise being the idling of the engine and the whirring of Dad's cine camera. We could hardly believe our eyes, we were spell-bound, oblivious of everything but LION. Thankfully the lions were equally oblivious of us!

Gradually they ate their fill and, with distended stomachs, moved away from the carcase. One lion, having thoroughly licked his face and paws, turned towards us and, with an upward flick and a swing of his tail, walked down into the watercourse, disappearing amongst the reeds, the tall grasses waving as he pushed his way through. Another left the kill and, with head carried low and jowl slightly open, had a good look at the car, then walked solemnly past it. If we'd ventured to put a hand out we could easily have stroked his back.

Two more came away, one paused to look back, head low, thinking very hard, wondering whether he'd had enough; then they walked away slowly and with great dignity, their coats glossy in the sunshine, and flopped down in the shade of a thorn tree. The last one then turned towards us. He took some time, too, to make up his mind if he'd had enough, pausing on his way to think it over. Then he came straight towards the car, nearer and nearer, glaring straight at us. Dad was filming all the time as he came up close, so close that all he could get in the view-finder was one of his eyes.

The jackals grew bolder, circling round agitatedly until the last lion had moved away and at last they could run in and clean up all the remains.

From Kruger Park, as from another world, we had to traverse back into civilization again – very reluctantly after the wonderment of being in the wilds and seeing these magnificent creatures in their natural state, at such close range. We motored back below Ship Mountain, one of the land-marks in the Park, and followed down the old Lyndenburg to the Lourenço Marques waggon route. This territory, now re-named the Tritchardt Road, had formed the background to FitzPatrick's classic *Jock of the Bushveldt*.

The *Llandovery Castle* docked at Lourenço Marques early in the morning and we found our cabins – not without a sigh of relief that we could fling open our suit-cases and install ourselves for a continuous month's voyage. After a farewell 'sun-downer', Peter had to leave us here to return to being a policeman at Rusapi, his rather envious sisters leaning on the deck-rail to bid him *au revoir*.

Farewell cards had been designed by Dad and we'd had these printed ready to take on board with us. The busy daughter-secretaries had their heads down, in their cabin-cum-office, addressing endless envelopes and by the time the ship had called in at Durban, East London, Port Elizabeth, and was approaching Cape Town, we had just about completed the list. When we went ashore at Capetown and stuffed them into a letter-box in Adderley Street, we could barely force them all in. These cards seemed to give such pleasure to the recipients and were far more appreciated than formal, stilted letters, typed by his two secretaries would have been.

Before we left the Cape the Chief Scout was anxiously trying to clinch the selection of a new Chief Commissioner and at the same time he put in one final hectic morning's work, having interviews with no less important personages than Sir William Clark (High Commissioner for the three Protectorates – Bechuanaland, Swaziland and Basutoland); Sir Cecil Fforde, General Smuts, General Hertzog and Mr Hoffmeyer.

Many more passengers had come on board now we were heading for Southampton, twenty-one days away. The ship was soon standing on her head and performing all sorts of antics as we came out of harbour and straight into a fine Atlantic swell. Just what Dad enjoyed and he stood on deck watching – not for the first time – Table

Mountain glowing in the evening sunshine as it faded slowly in our wake.

I am not sure how much Betty was acting a part or what indifference she at first felt, but she managed to pretend to be quite oblivious of the attentions of Gervas Clay. His parents had travelled out to South Africa to join him for this voyage home on six months' leave from Northern Rhodesia. As a District Officer he had been stationed in a very remote region of Barotseland.

He retaliated with a seemingly nonchalant attitude, although he usually managed to be going down to the dining saloon at the same time, or taking a deck chair up on the same Boat Deck; happening by chance to be reading in the Library or busily writing at a desk – not an adjacent desk but right across the lounge – where Betty happened to be writing her diary. Once back in England the courtship was cleverly conducted however, for by taking her to visit the romantic surroundings of his old College at Oxford, he persuaded her to marry him.

It put my parents in a bit of a quandary. Should they really agree to the marriage of their daughter, aged only just nineteen, to somebody she'd met but a couple of months ago who would take her to live in Darkest Africa? Yet how could they say no! The coincidences were too many and too similar to be ignored, for after all, had they themselves not first met on board ship – did they not share a mutual birthday?

After Dad had had one or two sleepless nights, and then a long talk with Gervas in the study, all was joy and the wedding was arranged for the very end of September so that their honeymoon could be spent on board ship with Gervas taking his youthful bride back with him to Africa. Invitations were written and despatched; a retinue of bridesmaids and little pages was gathered; there were frequent scurryings to London for dress fittings; a marquee went up on the lawn at Pax and amongst Dad's cheque-book stubs was found the entry 'Fizz for Betty's wedding' – and as more acceptances were received, 'More Fizz for Betty's wedding'.

As Dad was escorting Betty to the church from the front door of Pax, a swirl of wind blew her veil over him too. 'I don't know why all you brides ever need bother about wedding dresses,' he complained, disentangling himself from a cloud of tulle, 'when you've got all these veils and bouquets in front and more veils and long flowing trains behind!'

The Dean of Westminster gave the address, backed by a bus-load of choirboys, the organist and the Precentor from Westminster Abbey, and the little church of Bentley nearly raised its roof as they swelled into 'Lead us Heavenly Father, lead us.' As William Foxley Norris, the Dean had been a Carthusian friend of B-P – friend and rival, for both had artistic talent and when both competed for the coveted Leech Prize one year, Foxley Norris won it and B-P's painting only took second place. Dad's was a water-colour sketch of the main block of Charterhouse School, the light stone of the buildings standing out against a dark background of a threatening thunder-cloud. In a gold frame, it used to hang over the washstand in his dressing-room at Pax.

After the service we repaired to Pax where a marquee on the lawn below the house was waiting for the hundreds of guests who were to help in disposing of the 'Fizz for Betty's Wedding' and the 'more fizz for Betty's wedding'. Sir Alfred Pickford, an old friend of the family and a member of the Scout Headquarters Council, proposed the toast to the bride and bridegroom; then all too soon it was over and away went the happy couple to spend their honeymoon on board ship bound for Africa.

Pax had already had marquees on the lawn that summer, for garden parties were almost an annual event – and a very popular one. We had been busy with preparations for some time; Dad was hardest at work, repainting the lowered flag-staff and the white garden-seats; dark green for the dog kennels, and by the steps on to the lawn were two little iron pigs as boot-scrapers which he painted black with white spots on one side, stripes on the other. Mum was busy stripping ivy off the trees down the drive where the cars were to be parked and if ever she had a moment to spare she'd fetch out of their aviary a pair of little ring-doves I'd given her that summer, kissing the backs of their soft necks as they perched on the back of her hand.

The three hundred or more guests duly arrived and milled about the garden or sought out cups of tea. Some ventured into the house where I ran the projector and kept a continuous show going of the films Dad had taken in Africa. Mrs Wade acted as policeman on point duty, steering them in off the lawns where the elegant high heels sank deeply into the turf.

I probably had more than my fair share of attention this summer too, as my twenty-first birthday did not pass by unnoticed. In London my parents gave a large dinner party before we all went to the theatre. Afterwards they slipped away to their favourite Rubens Hotel while we young ones went dancing into the small hours, ending up at the Hungaria.

Next day, while out for a walk along Pall Mall with my father, he casually said 'Let's go in here'. I followed him as he turned in at the door of Hardy's shop, and ten minutes later I followed him out again, with a beautiful three-jointed trout rod tucked under my arm. This was not all. Driving him home from London later that week, we were slowing down at the entrance to Pax when he said 'Drive straight on for a bit', and directed me through Alton to Tom Downman's yard where a lovely chestnut hunter was led out for me to try. A bit wayward she proved to be, but I didn't mind that – in fact I rather liked it, there was a challenge. Our ginger-haired 'manes' matched and Dad said 'Do you think she'll do?' Speechless, and glowing with immeasurable delight, I squeezed my father's hand.

And now, he thought, perhaps I'd like to try out my new trout rod? In the midst of all his London commitments, he made time to snatch a

few days off and we sped away to Wales. Bear had given me lessons a year or two ago on driving Jam-Roll, and now Dad had 'handed over the reins' almost entirely to me. We took the silver fleur-de-lys Scout badge off the bonnet and substituted a humbler radiator-cap and drove off into the blue, incognito.

Somewhere near Ffestiniog we found the Oakley Arms and booked in as 'Major Pryor and his daughter' – Major *Beresford*-Pryor we quickly corrected on seeing the hall-porter looking sideways at the initials on the luggage. It was ever difficult for my father to be incognito, somebody always recognized him – someone who had been a Scout and had seen him at a Rally, a Camp, a Jamboree. 'That's what comes of being so ugly,' he would reply, shaking them warmly by the left hand.

CHAPTER ELEVEN

1937

'I'm an oxo-genarian' Dad gleefully declared as we came into the year 1937 and he set off on his travels again. This time the destination was India, with two main purposes in view; first to attend an all-India Scout Jamboree being held at Delhi, and secondly to pay a final visit to his Cavalry Regiment before it became mechanized, stationed up in the north at Risalpur, and formally to present them with new Drum Banners.

We left by a P&O ship from Tilbury as before, but this time the 'Official Party' had a few changes in its team, Lawrence and Joan Impey now replacing the Waltons and as Betty had 'defected' to Northern Rhodesia with her husband Gervas, we had gathered up Rosalind de Renzy-Martin to come in her place.

Landing at Bombay, my parents were welcomed with garlands and then had to attend official meetings, speak with the Press and have formal talks before stepping on to the Frontier Mail for Delhi. Here we stayed in a great state of comfort and were given a suite in the expansive, Lutyens-designed Vice-regal Lodge, with the Viceroy, Lord Linlithgow. Not only was the Jamboree taking place but it was followed by the Horse Show Week in Delhi, with its attendant Polo Tournament, the Delhi Hunt Ball, the Horse Show Ball, the Viceroy's Ball – there was some sort of dance or ball or carnival every evening, it seemed.

Flags were fluttering from a forest of tall white flag-poles as the Jamboree opened with a camp of 5,000 Scouts gathered here from all parts of India. There was a most colourful march past, the Scouts all in different coloured pugarees; everywhere around the camp they'd made decorative gateways and laid out gardens depicting their particular State. From Kashmir they'd come, Orissa and Bengal, the United Province, Madras, Mysore; there was a contingent from Ceylon and even one troop from Assam.

Dad was longing to see once more some of the old landmarks, from the days when he'd been a serving officer here – Delhi Fort with its massive red walls, the golf course with an ancient temple at every green. We took a drive out to the lovely

The Lord Chamberlain is commanded by Their Majesties to summon Lieut. General Lord & Lady Baden-Powell & Hon. Heather Baden-Powell to a Court at Buckingham Palace on Friday the 12th May, 1933, at 9.30 o'clock p.m.

Ladies: Court Dress with feathers and trains.
Gentlemen: Full Court Dress.

C43

_____ COURT PRESENTATION _____

Switzerland, 1931

*Dad with his 'Black Box',
presented by George Eastman
of 'Kodak'*

Malta Jamboree, 1933

Awaiting Audience with the Pope – the Ambassador, Mr Kirkpatrick, left

SWITZERLAND, MALTA AND ROME

pool at Oklah where we watched kingfishers and other brightly coloured birds diving after fish, and to Purana Kila, the old fort on rising ground above the Jumna River. We came back by Humayan's Tomb and drove slowly down the Chandni Chowk, the narrow street thronging with people and shopkeepers' wares and the sacred cows, white, hump-backed and emaciated, wandering at will, in the heart of Old Delhi.

We went southwards to Agra on the Punjab Mail Train (but it took four hours to cover 120 miles) and we didn't see the Taj Mahal by moonlight – rather dramatically we saw it in thunder and lightning instead. We wandered in and around it and watched tortoises in the Jumna; sat in the gardens and gazed at the outside, then went in to see the wonderful inlay work of flowers on the tombs of Shah Jehan and his beloved wife. Rain, torrential heavy rain, followed the thunderstorm and we made tracks quickly to leave Agra and return to Delhi.

From Delhi our party split off in different directions, to be reunited at Lahore a month later. Mum, with Rosalind at her side to attend Guide functions, set off to the south to start her tour from Madras heading northwards. Lawrence Impey, taking a load of engagements off Dad's shoulders, carried out a tour of Scouting duties in Central India, whilst Dad was able to revert back to his military life and go and 'join' his Regiment for a week in the Northern Frontier Province, taking me with him to Risalpur.

We had included in our luggage a pair of Drum Banners – pale blue silk background to the gold embroidered badge – given by Queen Mary to be presented to her Regiment, the 18th Hussars, of which she was Honorary Colonel. This Regiment and that of the 13th Hussars (of which Dad was Honorary Colonel) had some time ago been amalgamated. At a review at Aldershot some years previously when the Cavalry Regiments were to carry out a ride past together, it was debated who should ride at the head of which Regiment. 'Ma'am,' said the junior Honorary Colonel to the other, 'could we not ride together?'

We boarded the Frontier Mail which bore us northwards throughout the night and on again all next day, through mile upon mile of endless flat country. Breakfast at Lahore and on past Jhelum and Rawalpindi, reaching journey's end when we crept into Nowshera at dusk. Here Sidney Kennedy and his wife, Jane, stood waiting to take us along to the Commanding Officer's bungalow in the modern cantonments of Risalpur – colloquially known as Grizzly-paw.

Here, on his eightieth birthday, my father once again went on parade, mounted, with his old regiment, to present them with the new Drum Banners on behalf of Queen Mary. He had brought no military uniform with him, so Sidney lined up the most slim-built of his officers (Dad being of such slight stature himself) in order to borrow a uniform to fit. A placid charger was brought round for him to ride out on to the parade-ground, where he stood at attention while the presentation took place and the Banners, with the Regimental crest and 'Q.M.O.' embroidered in gold, were laid onto the drums carried on either side of the huge piebald drum-horse.

The band played and the whole regiment formed up for a march past. At the end of the parade ground they wheeled round and came thundering by at full gallop, truly a cavalry charge. It was a stirring moment for my father and his heart leapt as for a brief interlude he became a cavalry officer once again.

There were other old battlegrounds he was anxious to revisit, notably the Khyber Pass leading through into Afghanistan. Accompanied by several people from his regiment, a whole party of us set off in convoy, first to Peshawar, forty miles along a straight, tree-lined road, and from there Brigadier Molesworth led us on past Jamrud Fort where we entered the steep, bare hillsides of the Khyber. We followed the winding road, studded with piquets and look-out posts of heaped-up sandbags, the old marching road, into Landi Khotal where we were all entertained to lunch at the Officers' Mess of the Dorsets, stationed in this God-forsaken spot. We had passed Shargai Fort, occupied by men of the 5th Gurkha Regiment and went right on down to Landi Khana, at the border post into Afghanistan.

What wild, forbidding country it was, but Dad was so enjoying seeing the glowering, unchanging mountains and remembering the skirmishes with the Afridis, those tribesmen who stole the regimental transport mules at night and murdered their mail runners and were forever having sniping feuds against their own neighbouring villages. When the British Army finally withdrew from Afghanistan in 1881, B-P had been in command of the escort who fired the salute as the flag was hauled down in Kandahar, and was therefore one of the last British officers to leave.

The Swat Valley was another place vivid in his memory which he wanted to touch upon again, if he had the opportunity. He had been at Chakdara in 1897, and whilst his troops were digging rain-trenches round their tents, one of them had found a Greek signet ring. This, they decided, was undeniable proof that Alexander the Great, when he came to find a route through into India, must have passed through the Swat Valley, here at the Chakdara Crossing.

He made another little sally from Risalpur, escorted (all in civilian clothes in these peaceful years) by Officers of 13th/18th Hussars, to Malakand and on to Chakdara beyond. We motored comfortably along a well-surfaced road to Mardan, where we were hospitably received at the Mess of the Guides Cavalry, and then followed the winding road leading up out of the plains and into the mountainous country about Malakand, with a magnificent view looking back on the plains below.

We were led into the Fort at Malakand where we were met by Colonel Ricketts, who commanded the Gurkhas here. They gave us all lunch before escorting us on down the other side, steeply down into the Swat Valley and to the old fort at Chakdara, commanding the Swat River crossing.

One felt that the harsh mountains and rugged country had not altered their features since Alexander the Great had passed this way.

On top of the formalities of the Drum Banner presentation, my father had a lively week of constant entertainment in Risalpur. It included going to a regimental dinner, a 'dining in' night, a cricket match of Officers v. Sergeants, watching the training and schooling of young, newly drafted-in Remount horses, seeing a boxing match (in an R.A.F. hangar) against a team from the H.L.I. Regiment stationed at Peshawar, and attending a sergeants dance. He was quite forgetting he'd just had his eightieth birthday!

It seemed that I went to dinner parties every evening too, and also had no less than three early morning hunting days with the Risalpur Hounds, with Jimmy Hawker as Master and his wife, Joyce, the most knowledgeable member of the 'field'. Colonel Kennedy lent me his grey, Bluebird, and with about thirty-five mounted followers, we went hunting jackal across the flat, bush-studded plains beyond the airfield, or in the reed-beds along the Kabul River. Dad had been following the hunt in a car and we came back by Skinner's Nullah, exhausted but exhilarated after galloping for miles and miles, and now hacking gently back to stables through the tall yellow grassland.

'You mustn't go on to Pathankot tonight,' they advised in Lahore, 'the Dak bungalow there is filthy!' We had come jolting back in the train from the north at the end of a wonderful week for my father, immersed in memories of his 'previous' life – his military life No. 1 – but now jolted back into the reality of his Scout life, or Life No. 2.

Pausing here in Lahore, Mr Hogg seized upon the opportunity to take the Chief Scout out to Montmorency Park for the opening of a new swimming bath and to see the beautiful site the Movement had recently acquired in part of this large parkland, for camping and training in Scoutcraft.

By evening we were boarding a train again, heading eastwards this time, towards the Himalayas. The fishing rods hadn't come into play yet; Dad had not had his self-allowed fishing fee since the Jamboree at Delhi in February. Mr Grant Govan had long been tempting him with the offer of his bungalow in the Kulu Valley 'for as long as you would like to have it', and although it was early in the season and the fish scarce, it was an offer too tempting to decline.

So we now arrived by train at Pathankot in the early morning and were met by car to drive on another seventy-five miles by a beautiful road up to Palampur, below the snows. Here we stayed a night amongst tea plantations, at a bungalow belonging to an Indian lady doctor. Mr Guiton, who had made the arrangements for us, led us out for a stroll in the fresh mountain air, by a path through pine trees, to catch a glimpse of the remote little village of Llhana, tucked away in a smiling valley. In the evening he fascinated us with his enthralling stories of Yogis and snakes and of his adventures when he had gone climbing over into Tibet up to an altitude of 20,000 feet.

Kulu was still a long way ahead and soon after leaving Palampur we entered the State of Mandi. The road was no longer tarmac; it wound in and out of terraced hills and along narrow mountain ledges for a hundred miles, up to Mandi itself, and there were many delays on the one-way traffic system.

After crossing the rampaging Beas River the road became even more precarious, with the river deep down below and the threat of landslips and falling boulders after torrential rain the day before. Coolies were at work clearing the road of rubble washed down from above, and we were quite thankful when the last forty miles of the journey were completed and we reached Kulu. But the fishing bungalow was still another sixteen miles further up the valley and we were advised not to try to go on but to wait until the following day. More heavy rain fell during the night and we were getting anxious lest we'd never reach our goal. Reports had come in of washaways caused by the melting snows and that the road was still impassable. Later in the day, however, we heard it was possible to proceed and we pressed on up to Katrain. Here we were waylaid, even in this remote spot in the mountains, by a little group of Scouts gathered at the roadside. Mr Grant Govan's bungalow was not far ahead and we arrived at last at his retreat, set amidst the most magnificent scenery, with a flowing river below and endless snow-covered mountains above.

Thankful to have survived this somewhat hair-raising journey, we relaxed to enjoy a week lost in the atmosphere of eternal snows. The fishing came only second to the enjoyment of the scene; the water was dashing, fast and grey from the melting ice and snow, the boulders in the Beas river large and rolling, and the fish not keen. We caught a few small trout, particularly from a stretch of water above the Trout Hatchery at Katrain, where there were some good pools within easy reach of the road.

Back into civilization once more, we came winding our way down out of the mountains and gorges, leaving Mandi at Gottar Gate, into the Kangri district. Near Palampur we passed through a curious haziness which was caused by the pollen blowing off the deodar trees.

At Lahore we were reunited with our Official Party and found Mum in the midst of a garden party and Guide Rally; Dad had much to discuss with Lawrence Impey who had reports ready for him about all his visits. Rosalind and I were at work on our typewriters, until the Governor's A.D.C.'s came along and told us we were wanted outside. Moans and groans, we expected to find Press men wanting an interview, but instead we found ourselves being bundled into their shooting brake to go out snipe-shooting! The car was loaded with guns, food, drink, and all manner of changes of clothing, and off we went for about forty miles, to a watery *jheel*, abounding in snipe and wild duck. We waded through water and crept gingerly through the mud and reeds and

there seemed to be millions of birds – waders and water-fowl – wherever we looked. We had a marvellous day, pretending to be water spaniels.

Before leaving Lahore, Dad wanted to have a glimpse at the cathedral and the museum. His half-brother, Baden Henry Baden-Powell, his senior by sixteen years, had been in the Indian Civil Service most of his life and had become a judge here in the Punjab. When he died, he left all his money to these two great interests in his life – the cathedral and the museum. 'I wish he'd left me a bit,' Dad said, just a little ruefully, thinking how well an endowment for the Scouts' ground in Montmorency Park could have been used.

One more official occasion yet to fulfil! A big Scout Rally awaited us at Jaipur where we drove through the spaciously wide streets within the double city walls. At Amber, elephants were standing by, waiting to carry us up to the beautiful old palace – uninhabited for the last 200 years – on top of the hill. The young Maharajah of Jaipur, one of the most brilliant polo players ever to be seen, came to greet my father and bid him welcome, and then we were climbing up ladders again on to more elephants to ride up a paved way over a pass to see the old Temple of the Springs at Gulta.

Perhaps the choicest morsel on the plate had been kept till the last. Before journeying back to Bombay to catch the boat to England, we had a most memorable – and for my father a most nostalgic – week at Meerut to witness the annual pig-sticking competition for the Kadir Cup. 'Next to murder,' my father had researched, 'pig-sticking is one of the oldest sports in the world.' At the end of his book, *Pig-sticking or Hog-hunting*, he had written: 'If I am wanted after leaving this world, please call me up at Number One, Koila Jheel Muttra'. He'd often said that this was his spiritual home, and that's where he'd be found, back in his old happy hunting grounds, out on an Indian plain. (But that was a long time ago and before he had discovered the Outspan at Nyeri.)

Now, however, we were being taken by the Lumleys to renew memories of this, his sporting paradise, out in the plains north-east of Delhi, where wild boar abound. Tent Clubs at Muttra and Meerut, as well as many other places in India, organized pig-sticking competitions every year, the season being from March to July. A dangerous and most exciting sport, the competitors rode forth, either in threes or fours, with an Umpire, to find, then hunt the pig and finally kill it with a long spear. The pig were to be found mostly in jungly coarse grass where there were surprises and hazards such as water-conduits, walls made of dried mud, sunken lanes or 'bumbas' where local land-workers drove their oxen while drawing up water from wheel-headed wells; earth banks with irrigation runnels along the top; huge tufts of tiger grass, melon beds and 'nullahs' or dried out water-courses, deep and wide with steep sides and criss-crossed with goat tracks.

The horses they rode were for the most part Arabs, being the most adaptable to the treacherous ground, with their cat-like agility and short stride.

The Australian 'walers' were bigger and stronger but not so handy; the English thoroughbreds pretty useless, as, though faster, their legs and feet didn't stand up to the hard ground. 'C.B.s' or Country-breds, indigenous to India, were the easiest and cheapest to get hold of and could be found, as my father wrote, 'in every size and shape and certainly in every colour of the equine species.'

Every year since 1867 (excluding 1915–18, the years of War) the Kadir Cup was competed for by members of the various Tent Clubs, and run off in heats. In 1883 Dad himself had qualified with two of his best pig-sticking horses (both mares) and got through to the finals. As he obviously couldn't ride both, he got his friend and brother officer 'Ding' MacDougall to ride Patience and he himself took Hagarene (or 'Gangrene' as one of his compatriots always called her). Perhaps the best description of what happened next comes from his own words:

How I did NOT win the Kadir Cup

Such excitement! Twenty elephants with onlookers, fellows up in trees and others riding their horses to see the fun. Away went a great boar in front of us – 'Ride!'

Away we went after him. Hagarene drew away from the rest as she was tremendously fast and keen. The pig dashed across open ground into a very thick, coarse jungle, but I was pretty close to him and could just see him every now and then through the great tussocks of grass six feet high. Hagarene bounded through them like a motor-boat in a big sea; then across twenty yards of open ground and into another patch of jungle, even thicker than before and steeply banked. Once she pecked and we were very nearly down. One of the tussocks had a solid pillar of hard earth in it which the mare struck with her chest, but she managed to recover herself. Now we were close on to him and I got my spear ready to reach out and give him the winning thrust. At that moment a green hedge appeared in front and almost as the pig disappeared through it Hagarene cleared it and there, ten feet below, was the shining surface of the river!

The pig went plump in under water and Hagarene and I did the same, almost on top of him. Right down we went under water, down and down into the depths! A deal of struggling, striking out, swimming in heavy clothes and boots, till eventually, with the aid of weeds and bushes, I pulled myself out on the far bank and saw Hagarene clambering out too a few yards away and off she went, full split for camp. The pig meantime had turned and swum back to where he'd entered the water, creeping up among the reeds. As the other men in the heat came up to the hedge and looked over, I pointed out the pig and away they went on his new line. MacDougall was the first to reach him on Patience and, spearing him hansomely, won the Cup for me.

Aden

Colombo

On the bridge of the 'Orama'

Thursday Island Scout Troup

Java

March past, 16 abreast, Australian Jamboree

WORLD TOUR

Crossing the Bela River, New Zealand

Tahiti

Investing Mum with the name 'Otter Woman', Calgary

With our grateful Thanks

Au Revoir

U.S.A.

NEW FOUND LAND

Baden Powell

Heather Olave Baden Powell.

Betty

New York skyline

1934–35

A funny object I looked when the others came up to congratulate me, dripping with mud and water and garlanded with green weeds, but the happiest man among them.'

(from *Indian Memories*)

The Cup that Patience won that day, with its handles formed from the tushes of the pig, is now cherished in the home of B-P's grandson, Robert, whose wife's name, appropriately enough, is Patience.

That was in 1883 – now it was 1937 and from the back of an elephant my father could savour once again the thrill of seeing a wild boar break cover from the jungle and hear the soul-stirring cry to 'ride' to get first spear.

'What do we have to wear?'

'Whose are the elephants we ride on?'

'Who gives the signal to start?'

'Where will they find a pig?'

'How many heats will they run?'

Before leaving Muttra we, the uninitiated, were anxiously plying our hosts, the Lumleys, with these questions; Dad, silent with anticipation, knew the answers to them all.

We followed a long, dusty road to Ghar and crossed a stretch entirely covered by smooth sand, to reach the Bridge of Boats. Here was a small village of straw huts built on the banks of the Ganges. Outside the houses were hanging bottles filled with holy Ganges water for sale; the richer man could come and select the champagne bottles.

We crossed the flat pontoons and came into the shade of trees along the Hafeeze road and outside this high-walled village was an arch of Welcome with flags hung out in readiness for the arrival of the Viceroy, and a signpost said 'To Kadir Cup'. Further on was another arch of Welcome and signs to 'Collectors' Camp' and to 'Ladies Camp' (or Bagh). Through a belt of trees there was a great circle of tents, with paved pathways to the Mess Tent and chairs arranged out in the middle. No hog-hunters, spears, elephants or horses about – just a few dust-covered cars and two sleepy, trouser-clad girls having tea brought to them by an Indian bearer. A notice here said 'No horses to be brought into the Bagh – they cause flies.'

We were brought tea too, and then drove over to the Men's Bagh all in the shade of trees and accommodating nearly 100 competitors and their supporters. Dad wondered if they'd forgotten the grandfather clock, so elaborate was the camp, with dressing tables, bathrooms, rush mat 'carpets' and wooden 'sharpoy' beds.

Another half-mile on through a field of barley, where a gang of local coolies were cutting a way along the side, we came to the Horse Bagh. Rows of horses were tied up, heads to tails, standing in deep bedding, bandaged and fly-netted and being fed with freshly cut grass. Their *syces*, or grooms, were tending them, carrying water buckets, cleaning saddlery and some dressing the wounds from this morning's first rounds, of which eighteen heats had already been run.

Troop horses from 17th/21st Lancers stood in

their lines; some had their names written above and one difficult customer was penned in with taut ropes all round him as though he were a boxer. Much excited gossip and speculation went on after the morning's results; Manifest was not the favourite, Lindy Lou was out of it with colic and 'Elbow' Elliot had won a most spectacular spear, riding his second horse, Dinah.

The Elephant Bagh was another quarter-mile further out; some of them were gathered round a pump, being given drinks or having buckets of water thrown over them by their mahouts, after which they picked up dust in their trunks and powdered themselves or scratched themselves with branches which they snatched off the trees in passing back to their lines. In the lines they were being fed sugar-cane, their forefeet chained together and a larger chain anchoring them by one hind leg. Their names and ages were written up on a little flag by their chains; elephants of all different shapes and sizes, and all with different expressions – thirty-two in all. Most of them had been lent by nabobs and Indian potentates, well-wishers of pig-sticking, and there was one small elephant who strung along so closely to its mother that the spectators who were riding it complained the only view they had had was of the backside of the mother elephant.

On our way back to the Visitors' Bagh, we ladies had carefully to detour the Men's Bagh – strict segregation of the sexes here! In the most civilized manner of Camping, we changed for dinner. Bathed and dressed, and wearing coats against the cool night air, we dined in a huge, long tent, by the light of Petrolux lamps. Most of the conversation revolved round the day's heats and the six horses which had been injured on their train journey here. Tales from the past were related too; the umpire who'd escaped death from a charging boar and won his spear, only to be killed by an elephant as he was dismounting it soon after. How Manifest had fallen while closing on a boar but then stood stock still and waited close by till 'Friar' Tuck was able to remount.

Afterwards we went across to the main camp to listen to the draw for tomorrow's heats, and to hear the official results of today's events, which were hailed by bursts of cheering or moans of teasing disapproval. We went to our beds to the sound of chorusing frogs and the distant beating of drums at an Indian village wedding.

Next day we rode out on the elephants, our mobile grandstands, to watch the final heats for the Kadir Cup. We were classed as V.I.P.'s and were put on an elephant carrying a howdah, but most others were saddled with enormous mattress-like pads. We wobbled out of camp in single file to Sujmana and after fording a deep nullah we spread out in line abreast, the competitors cantering up and down ahead of us. In front of them went the coolies, or beaters, banging and shouting their way through the long grass. Behind us came the *pani wallahs* or water carriers, and the horses which were to compete in later heats, being led along by their syces. The Field Master was on the leading or flag elephant, with shikaris on camels riding out on either flank and the umpires with white flags controlling each heat as they awaited the order, on the rousing of a boar, to *Ride*.

At the drop of the umpire's flag, away they'd gallop; it was often impossible for us spectators to see the pig (as fox-hunters often can't see the fox) but the riders we could just see – topees and spears and sometimes the backs of their horses, bobbing through the jungle. All went still and silent when a 'spear' had been made and the shikaris went in to carry back the dead boar. The next heat then rode forward to take up their position ahead of our elephants, watching for pig, and for the fall of the umpire's flag. These moments my father relived with what he called 'an almost sickening feeling of suspense'.

John Adye sighted a pig at one moment, just as an umpire was going out after another with his heat; one of the elephants started trumpeting loudly – a pig had broken back behind the line. The riders turned and came galloping back through a herd of somewhat surprised native cattle and eventually David Barbour got a spear to it after plunging through a muddy river where Captain Graham's horse had come down.

We had another sensational moment when a panther, a very large and angry panther, was disturbed from its grassy bed and broke back behind us. The Field Master ordered the whole line of us on our elephants to turn ourselves about and any spare riders and umpires quickly grabbed their spears. After wounding one of these horses, the panther galloped along in full view and then lay crouching in the grass, waiting to pounce at anybody who dared to come within range. Eventually one of the A.D.C.'s speared him but not before he had sprung out and gashed his horse's chest with its fearsome claws.

The final heat was fought out between A. Brandon on Red Turk and D. Barbour on Uncle Bourh Gunga (won by Red Turk) and as we rode back to camp after it was all over, we observed the rules: 'Do NOT race your Elephants back to Camp. Do NOT bandage horses' legs till after crossing deep Nullah'. In the Horse Bagh there was much veterinary activity, some worthy wounds, 'big' legs and hot tendons demanding attention and much anxious trotting up and down, knowing nods of wise heads, watching for lameness or pain.

After the 'sickening feeling of suspense' my father had referred to and the excitement of the whole day, I felt very sick as I slid to the ground. The hot sun beating down on us and the swaying walk of the elephant had made me feel sea-sick – and although I felt quite sorry for myself, it was my poor father who felt far worse through the night than I.

From his bed, next day, Dad took up his pen and wrote to Mrs Wade:

Meerut, 21 March '37

Dear Mrs W.

We have just had another red-letter day in our lives! We four have been out to see the Kadir

Cup run, for three days. Yesterday was the final, over 100 of us on thirty elephants, from 9 a.m. to sunset, out on a vast yellow grass plain – the whole day under blazing hot sun, wobbling along on elephants with the excitement of watching the competitors racing after pig and, in one case, hunting and killing a panther. Then a 48-mile motor ride home over bumpy tracks to late dinner at nine. To bed at eleven. From 11.30 till 5, violently sick until I had nothing left to be sick with! From 5 a.m. till now, 5 p.m., I've been asleep. Now having tea and going to bed again so as to be fit tomorrow to travel to Delhi and see the Viceroy – and then on 23rd on night train to Bombay.

Awfully sorry to leave India and all its happy memories.

But he quickly recovered and taking a dusty train we arrived in Bombay in time to board the S.S. *Maloja* for the return journey to a cold English April.

CHAPTER TWELVE

1937

We were back in England in time for an endless chain of events, the most colourful being the processions and pageantry for the Coronation of King George VI and Queen Elizabeth; flags everywhere and sight-seers in their thousands flocking to London, if only to see the decorations on Selfridges.

Throughout the country the bunting was hung out; we joined in at Pax, festooning the walls at the entrance to the drive. Then we quickly returned to the house to help dress up Mum and Dad and despatch them in Jam-roll, sitting bolt upright in all their finery of ribbons and sashes of Orders and Garters, to attend a State Banquet. Twenty-four hours earlier, Dad had been in the river saving Shawgm from drowning! He was out fishing down below Anstey Bridge on the river Wey and Shawgm, by now grey-muzzled and a little blind, was pottering along the bank when he fell in; Dad had quickly to drop his rod and wade into deep water to pull the poor old labrador out.

The State Banquet wasn't the only occasion for which my parents were invited to Buckingham Palace during this summer. Dad had been awarded the Order of Merit in the Coronation Honours list – an honour held by only twenty-four other people – 'in appreciation of his valuable services to the Empire', and was requested to receive it personally at the hands of the new King during an informal chat in his study. Four days later, at the end of May, there was a Court Ball at which we were able to stand on some steps quite near to the thrones and watch the Royalty dancing in their own little 'pen'.

On 22nd June they attended – along with ten thousand other guests – a Royal Garden Party. Already that same morning my father had taken Sidney Kennedy, Colonel of the 13th/18th Hussars to attend a Levee at St James's Palace, in all the glory of their full dress uniform.

Whenever my father had a nightmare – though this was not a frequent occurrence – it was always the same dream: he was going to some formal occasion but exasperatingly found that he was wearing the wrong dress. This could well have happened over the past couple of months, as there had been such a variety of occasions when he had called upon every change of uniform he possessed.

The Royal Family gave much time and attention to Scouting and Guiding; they showed their appreciation and interest in many ways; by becoming patrons of the Movement, by personally attending functions and by letting the little Princesses, in their Brownie and Guide uniforms, have regular meetings of their own Pack and Company in the grounds of Buckingham Palace.

For Whitsun weekend, in glorious weather at Eastnor Park at the southern end of the Malvern Hills, there was a Scout gathering with 2,000 under canvas at the home of Lord Somers, the future Chief Scout. It was a magnificent setting, with the castle floodlit at night and a fire blazing on Beacon Hill. During Whit-Sunday, Guides came pouring into the camp too, four thousand strong, and held a Rally.

Later that week my parents went on board the large white liner, the *Strathmore*, to see the Naval Review, with warships anchored all along Spithead. They watched the royal yacht sail up and down between the lines of the Mediterranean and Home Fleets, the visiting foreign warships and the Merchant Navy and fishing vessels, flags flying, dressed overall.

Turning from naval and military reviews, my father also took a great interest in the Royal Air Force and, with a boyish enthusiasm to start Air Scouts, went to watch a flying display at Hendon. I drove him over there in Jam-roll, but there was such a traffic jam outside that we couldn't get in at the gates. A fly-past of 240 aeroplanes had caused all cars to stop where they were, while everybody got out and rubber-necked. We saw upside-down aeroplanes bursting balloons with gun-fire; diamond-shaped formation flying; Hawker Hectors and Fairey Battles; aerobatic loops and rolls, and finally an attack on 'Fort Hendon' itself.

A telephone call came through to Pax one morning from a newspaper offering a tempting fee if Dad would give them an article entitled 'My Belief'. My father, the son of a parson, was certainly a devout man of God. As the leader of a movement embracing all denominations, it was only right that he showed no favouritism to any particular creed, though he himself had been brought up in the Christian faith as an Anglican. Few were the occasions when he was free to walk through the hop-fields and along the cart-track behind Jenkyn Place to attend Matins in Bentley Church; but many the Scouts' Own services which he attended in cathedrals, churches, chapels, and, most appreciated of all, the outdoor gatherings, terminating with prayers being offered under God's own sky.

Perhaps this would be a timely moment to quote the prayer he once wrote:

Dear Father of all, we thank Thee for the many blessings and much happiness which Thou hast granted us.

(Pause to think of these and to realize how well off you are compared with many others.)

For such blessings, deeds of thankfulness are,

Egypt

UNION-CASTLE LINE
S·S "LLANDOVERY CASTLE"

Mum on safari

Lion!

Me, writing the log

Jamboree at East London, and (inset) 'Gran' Walton

AFRICA, 1935–36

The Khyber Pass

Encampment, Kadir Cup, R.B-P.

Following the Kadir Cup

INDIA, 1937

in Thy sight, more acceptable than mere words of praise. Therefore shall we render our thanks by working in Thy cause and by doing that which is the truest service to Thee.

To this end, Oh God, help us by developing in us less of care for self and more of care for others.

Strengthen in us that love that binds us each to all and all to Thee, that through our brotherhood of Scouts, which under Thy good care has spread across the world, we may help to bring about the spirit of goodwill and peace between the nations.

So may Thy kingdom come and Thy will be done on earth as it is in Heaven.

His views on politics were just about as open-minded as those on religion. His one great sigh was 'If only our country could be run by Statesmen instead of Politicians it wouldn't be in the mess it is today.'

In mid-June came the news from Northern Rhodesia that Betty and Gervas had a daughter. I personally was rather cross with her, as one of my requests to her on her marriage was 'Please do not make me into an old aunt too quickly.' She hadn't listened!

In July I was invited to a dance given by the Carvers in Farnham which was destined to shape the rest of my life, for I met a young would-be accountant called John King whose parents I had met earlier in the year when staying in the Cotswolds with the Impeys. In October he came to

stay at Pax in his MG accompanied by a small dachshund whereupon he was dubbed 'the man with the long low car and the long low dog'. From then on we were to see more and more of each other.

In the meantime my sister got to know, before my parents, that Peter had secretly married that year, having met him and his wife Carine as they passed through Southern Rhodesia on their honeymoon. In October they had a son, to be christened Robert. The B.S.A. Police did not approve of Troopers being married until they reached promotion and so Peter had to keep it quiet until his transfer came through and he went into the Department of Native Affairs. He wrote the news home to my parents, which they received early in 1937, the very day we were leaving for India. The news was not exactly welcomed with pleasure at first, but they became very philosophical and were glad to know that this was bringing much happiness to him, embarking upon family life, obviously now settling in Rhodesia, in their beloved Africa. Peter and Carine had tried, it would seem, to repeat the family coincidences by having their son born on what was their joint birthday (and incidentally my parents' wedding day), 30th October, but Carine said a thunderstorm frightened her and Robert was born a fortnight too early.

Now there came for the Chief Scout his final Jamboree, and he above others felt that this was it – his Grand Finale.

It fulfilled this to the maximum degree with a gathering in Holland of 30,000 Scouts camping in the parkland and dunes of Vogelenzang, the ancient home of the Counts of Holland, not far from Haarlem. The huge contingent which came across from Britain was split up and scattered amongst the Scouts drawn here from all over the world to camp together in each of the ten sub-camps. The whole atmosphere was just as my father had intended it to be – a happy crowd of youngsters gathered together to make friends and understand one another. The weather, for once, behaved itself perfectly.

The badge they all wore as the symbol of this Jamboree was a Jacob's Staff – the mariner's guide of days gone by, with the four-pronged crosses in diminishing sizes down the staff. At the final parade replicas were handed out to each country taking part.

Each day Dad had made his way through a different section of the camp, closely guarded by the stern, sturdy figure of 'Belge' Wilson, the Camp Chief of Gilwell, firm as a bulldog defending his master. Also backing him up were two eminent pillars of Scouting, Prince Gustave Adolf of Sweden (later so tragically killed in an air distaster) and, as chief host, Prince Bernhardt of the Netherlands.

'Brother Scouts', the Chief began, speaking for the last time to such a multitude, 'the time has come for me to say good-bye. We have come to the end of our Jamboree; we are meeting for the last time – for some of us. I am in my 81st year and am nearing the end of my life . . . you are at the beginning of yours . . .', he hesitated momentarily, his voice full of emotion, and then continued, 'but in this there is no cause for melancholy, but rather the opposite; it is an occasion of thanksgiving for a very happy experience. Each one of you will carry away a different impression, according to his temperament, but all such impressions cannot fail to be happy ones, mainly of new revelations in Scouting, in its methods, in its possibilities and in new friendships and comradeships begun. . . . Through this goodwill let us help to bring about God's reign of peace among men. Good-bye, and God bless you all.'

Belge guided him safely back to the red car to drive away through the surging Scouts amidst their tumultuous singing – no matter in what language – of their theme-song, 'Jamboree, Oh, Jamboree!'

Jam-roll had clocked up quite a good milage this summer; apart from the frequent short runs to London (fifty miles exactly from Pax to Scout H.Q.) we'd made several long week-end journeys around England. To Birmingham for a Rally of 14,000 Scouts at Handsworth Park (with a detour to see the beautiful new camping place at Kinver); another week-end we motored up to Leicester for a Rally on the show-ground and from there, at racing speed to keep up with him, we followed the Duke of Rutland to stay at Belvoir Castle. On another occasion we went to Derby where the Bemroses had arranged for Dad to open an extension of land to the lovely Drum Hill in the Pennines – having been led to believe it was to be a quiet little affair, he was rather taken aback when ambushed by 1,400 cheering Scouts.

Now, at last, after the Jamboree, Dad was ready to get away on holiday – to Scotland. Through the Pass of Glencoe we drove and on to Oban. There was a tricky manoeuvre at the wharfside here, steering Jam-roll on to narrow planks which tipped up with the car like a see-saw as it ran on to the ferry *Lochinvar* to go across to Mull. Here Dad and I enjoyed a week's fishing. We hardly caught a fish – they seemed to be away on holiday too – it was getting late in the season. But that didn't detract from the enjoyment of the scenery and the relaxation at the riverside; the tranquillity of mountains and sea, rocky islands and deep bays.

The young man in a kilt who came down to Salen to welcome us ashore was Charles Maclean, grandson of Sir Fitzroy Maclean of Duart – 'Chips' he was called. I wonder what vision might have been passing through the minds of both of them that day as we drove by Craignure to Duart – the Chief Scout and the man who was to succeed him later.

Everybody seemed determined that Dad should get a fish, offering him the best stretches of water; the Bryce Allens' offered their beat on the Aros and the Mellis's said 'Come and try the sea-pools in the River Baa.' Colonel Gardiner suggested his loch in Glen More and Lady Scott sent us off down to Aros Bridge. But to no avail! We had our

mid-day picnics lying on burn-side banks in the bracken and heather, basking in the sun, and then in to tea with some nearby crofters. MacPhail, the ghillie, took us to lovely pools on General Maitland's water, but it was too low and clear and although we could see those idle salmon just loafing about enjoying themselves, never a touch did we get.

We hadn't long returned from Scotland when we heard the news that Dad's brother Baden was very ill after a heart attack, and so Mum and Dad sped over to Sevenoaks just in time to see him before he died. 'Dear, fat, lazy old Uncle Baden,' we used to chide him; he lived in his bachelor world amongst books and aeronautical magazines piled high in his stuffy little study. He had been a leading authority on ballooning, but being so shy and retiring, left others to gain the publicity of his revelations. Out in the greenhouse was the invention he was always working on, without success – a gun that could shoot round corners.

He was not at all unlike Dad to look at (except that he was so much fatter). There was one memorable moment of mistaken identity when Uncle Baden was sitting in the drawing-room at Pax reading *The Times* when Mum came in and gently went up behind him and lovingly kissed the back of his head.

A memorial service was held for him at the Guards' Chapel at Wellington Barracks. He had been a Major in the Scots Guards and had fought in the South African War. He was with the relief column which entered Mafeking – it was he who

was the first officer to burst in, to greet his own brother with the cry 'Mafeking is relieved!'

Uncle Baden, though younger than Dad (in fact the youngest of them all), was the last of his brothers to die; there was only his sister Agnes left. She was his senior by one year and had always been devoted to my father. She called him Stephie or 'Ste' from his second name, Stephenson, after his godfather, 'the steam-engine man'. He referred to her as Azzie or Az but we always called her Aunt Agnes, very sedately, and stood at attention when confronted. She came to stay at Pax quite frequently, but although we were quite fond of her she wasn't much fun; she didn't ride or play games. She had untidy, wispy red hair and blue stockings which, on her thin little legs, always appeared to be coming down. She was tiny in stature but made up for it by being quite large in importance in the early days of Guiding. In fact, she was the mainstay of the Movement at its inception. When Guides were first brought into being and Dad was faced with this awkward female problem which had surprisingly arisen, it was Aunt Agnes who flung herself, heart and soul, into her brother's enterprise and was therefore largely responsible for the founding of the Guide Movement in Britain.

Although a true Victorian, she must have had in her make-up something of the same genius which B-P had inherited from his forebears. She was a great naturalist and kept a number of small birds – and even bees – in her London house and induced the latter to produce prize-winning honey. There was hardly any handicraft in which she did not excel, and she was the expert President of Queen Alexandra's Needlework Guild in London. But when her brother turned to her for help in his unexpected development of Scouting – how to be adapted for girls – she readily faced the prejudices which at that time existed against any such feminine movement. A great fear existed that girls would be turned into 'tom-boys', or into those 'dreadful suffragettes', and would lose their maidenly modesty with their manners. Against any such fear Aunt Agnes was a safety-valve and no-one could have been better fitted to bring the idea of Guides gradually before an apprehensive public than this gentle Victorian lady.

When B-P married and his young wife introduced a more modern and youthful outlook into the girls' Movement, Agnes gradually subsided into a back seat, but it should never be forgotten that it was her influence which began, on this modest scale, something which later developed so widely throughout the world.

At the end of October, greetings telegrams started coming to the door of Pax by the handful, from all over the world. It was my parents' Silver Wedding. Not only telegrams, but presents of silver too, and all followed by a magnificent dinner party given for them at the Mayfair in London and attended by 300 Scout and Guide Commissioners from everywhere in Britain. Lord Somers proposed the toast and the chief guest, the Princess Royal, formally presented them with several beautiful pieces of silver as well as a cheque for over £2,000 which, she explained, was for them to buy 'some of those small domestic wants that are always felt in a household'. These wonderful presents could not have come at a more timely moment. There had been a burglary at Pax the year previously and several pieces of silver had been stolen, but it was gratifying that they could now be replaced, even if the sentimental value had been lost. 'They couldn't have been very good burglars, actually,' Dad had decided. They'd missed the main prize for which they had obviously come – the gold casket presented to him by the City of London a few days before. Luckily the doors of its case were shut, so it didn't gleam in the light of their searching torches. But they had seized eagerly upon Mum's little leather sewing-box, sitting in the drawing-room pretending to be a jewel case. On discovering the contents at their departure, they threw them away, leaving a trail of scissors, cotton-reels and bits of darning wool all down the drive. Poor old Shawgm, getting very crotchety and deaf now, and his days num-

bered, hadn't barked, having not heard a thing. Schofield, the gardener, was absolutely furious; he'd only bedded out the wallflowers that very day, and they'd gone and trampled on the lot, leaving their earthy foot-marks right across the lawn and on down the drive.

The second part of their Silver Wedding present was also most acceptable at this moment, not so much to buy household goods – but a whole house! A tiny little house in Kenya. When my parents had previously visited Eric Walker's Out-span Hotel, they had both completely fallen in love with it, and this was where they now wished to be. Eric had offered to build them a bungalow beyond the hotel – and here now was the money available for them to do so. Everything seemed to fall into place.

And so, at the end of this exhausting year, they were able to set sail for Kenya and relax into a retired winter at Nyeri, with wineberries and cream for breakfast.

CHAPTER THIRTEEN

1938

On the threshold of 1938 Dad must have been working on his theory that 'I've only three more years to live'. This had been his policy for living for a good many years and must have been the impulse which goaded him to drive himself on at the pace he did latterly. To achieve the tremendous amount of work he got through (a good deal of which was done before breakfast), combined with the continuous travelling from one end of the world to the other, helping to encourage and spread the spirit of the Scout Movement, he must have had Cecil Rhodes' dying words ringing in his ears: 'So much to do, so little time to do it'.

Mentally he was as alert as ever, but physically he was flagging and he had 'a tired heart' – specialists in Nairobi had ordered him to go slow and to take a year's complete rest.

When they left England to go to Kenya after their Silver Wedding my parents left me behind; they had no need of a daughter-secretary to accompany them, now they were obeying doctor's orders to go slow. Having given me a hunter, they left me in England to enjoy a season's hunting, staying with friends in Dorset and in Gloucestershire.

The previous October had seen the handing-over of the *Discovery* by the Duke of Kent, and amongst the guests was Lady Kennet, the widow of Captain Scott, with her son, Peter; she herself, as Kathleen Scott, was a well-known sculptress, and Peter already acknowledged as an ornithologist and painter of birds as well as a great dinghy helmsman. While we were all having tea in the wardroom my father had jokingly introduced me to Lady Kennet as his Deplorable Secretary for whom he had no more use – the outcome of which was a telephone call for me to go for interview and then to go and do secretarial work for her at their London house, Leinster Corner, with her studio across the garden. It was only to be a part-time job and while my parents were in Kenya this made it easy for me to whizz down to Pax during weekends where Mrs Wade had everything ready for their return in the Spring.

I had a disturbing letter from Mum in January,

saying that Dad had not been feeling at all well and 'had a bad go of lumbago'. She had had to cancel a trip they had planned to visit the Guides in South Africa, and also they were hoping to have seen both Peter and Betty on their way back north to Kenya. I wired back at once that I would fly out to them and immediately booked myself on to a flight to Nairobi. A cable came next morning however:

Loving thanks considerate suggestion but unnecessary as splendid steady improvement daily – MUM.

A letter followed saying that they would be coming back to England anyway, 'on a slow boat', in May. They came, slowly, in the old *Llangibby Castle*, stopping at several points down the east coast of Africa. When they called in at Beira, Peter seized the opportunity to get down to the Portuguese East African coast from Inyanga to see them. This was a joyous occasion for them, for not only did he bring Carine, his wife, to meet them for the first time, but also their eighteen-month-old grandson, Robert, whom Dad was able to pick up and hold wriggling in his arms.

Early on the morning of 21st May, Mrs Wade and I took Jam-roll down to the new docks and watched *Llangibby Castle* come up Southampton Water and turn herself round. As soon as she berthed we scurried up the gangway to greet them and bring them home. Dad seemed utterly exhausted and was glad to be able to rest quietly in the garden at Pax for days on end. I went for long walks with Mum and the dogs and we talked of future plans – which mostly consisted of how quickly they could get back to Africa!

A heart specialist in London pronounced the same diagnosis as the one in Nairobi – a tired heart and a year's rest. 'I could have told him that myself' Dad declared – but we wanted the assurance.

This advice didn't stop him going to London occasionally; he continued to attend Mercers' Company meetings on as many Fridays as he could, and one day he couldn't resist taking a walk along the Embankment to have a look at *Discovery* again. He went on board and, although incognito, he was promptly recognized and made to stay for lunch. He and Mum liked also to go to the theatre – they'd been to see *Robert's Wife* with Owen Nares as the vicar and Edith Evans as his fussing wife; *The Corn is Green, French without Tears* and *Good-bye Mr Chips*. One evening I joined him 'on the spree' and he took me to the Trocadero for oysters and stout.

At home he much enjoyed his glass of beer at lunch-time, and in the evening at dinner, a glass of wine, usually a white Bordeaux. Sometimes, if he was tired, he would have a whisky and soda. When I was small I can remember watching most anxiously when Florence the parlour-maid was pouring the whisky from a decanter, terrified that she would pour too much and 'make him drunk'.

In August we sailed away on the third of the Scouters' and Guiders' Cruises, due to call at four of the northern capitals of Europe. Dad's physique had grown no stronger and he was told by his doctors that he could only go on the cruise on condition that he didn't land anywhere, nor subject himself to being mobbed by Scouts and Guides.

This 'floating camp', as it was appropriately dubbed, took us out of Liverpool on a horribly foggy evening in mid-August, with incessant blowing of the fog-horn at regular half-minute intervals, all through our first night at sea. We dropped anchor two days later at Reykjavik where Icelandic Scouts and Guides came streaming up the gangway and climbed on board to greet us. They had arranged to lead us ashore and to accompany us, in twenty-eight bus-loads, sightseeing to Thing-vellir, the ancient gathering place of their Parliament, and also to drive 118 kilometres to Gullfoss through country not unlike Scotland, except that the open tracts of moorland were solid lava, supporting no vegetation whatever. There was a marvellous two-tier waterfall tumbling into a deep chasm and from there we were taken on to Geysir to see the new eruption which was supposed to occur at hourly intervals, but it refused to play, even after we'd waited for an hour and thrown in pounds of soap to stimulate it into action.

We crossed the North Sea into Norwegian waters and were eventually piloted up the fjord to the northerly town of Trondhjem (where the cathedral has a most magnificent rose window). Excursions were arranged to Grakollen to see the dizzy slopes of the ski-jumps, at the time bereft of snow; and to Lerfoss to see another spectacular waterfall (for Norway has no dearth of these). We returned in time for a Scout and Guide parade on the original site of the old Archbishop's Palace. At midnight, although hardly dark, we were gliding down Trondhjem fjord again, leaving the twinkling lights of civilization – though not those of the aurora borealis which we'd hoped to see – against the black, mountainous coastline.

Copenhagen, which we'd been unable to visit on the previous cruise owing to some political upheaval, gave us a terriffic welcome, despite the cold drizzle. We drove off in buses to see Hamlet's ramparts at Elsinore, to Frederiksborg, Friedensborg and Kronborg; some visited the Tuborg Brewery but it was not easy to try and sample the beer and fizzy drinks at ten o'clock in the morning.

At night it was so wet that an indoor 'camp-fire' was improvised in the Forum, 15,000 strong. If the weather had been kinder, it was to have been held out at the Dyrehaven where the 1924 World Jamboree had been held.

Next day, before we sailed in mid-afternoon, thousands of Scouts and Guides thronged the quay, singing and cheering and calling for their Chief. Dad went up on to the Captain's Bridge dressed in Scout uniform, and spoke to them all. He later summed up the cruise in these pencilled lines:

The Rhyme of the 'Orduna' Cruise

Starting on our third 'Peace Cruise'
Through foggy nights we boomed the news
And when at length to sea we stood
Neptune proved in kindliest mood.

First we came to Raykjavik
Scarce knowing what to make of it
But those folk of Northern seas
Set us promptly at our ease
With water-falls and well-soaped Geysers
They did their very best to please us.

Then to Norway, up a fjord
(Novel scene for all on bjoard)
At Trondjhem (Vikings' home of yore)
Four hours late we went ashore
Welcomes such as made us glad
But midnight partings made us sad.

Copenhagen, there the Dane
Welcomed us with flags – and rain.
Camp-fires, tours and Elsinore,
Feasts and friendliness galore.

Bless the hearts and smiling faces
Of those Scandinavian races!

War-clouds were rolling during September 1938; Soldiers were recalled to their regiments and gas-masks were issued to every citizen in the land. Tension mounted as we heard of German troops flocking to the Czech border; Hitler's speech was broadcast and everyone felt keyed up for the announcement of war. What a flood of relief when we heard that the leaders of the four Powers had met at Munich – Hitler, Mussolini, Chamberlain and Daladier; the crisis seemed to have been averted.

Clare, poor Clare Davidson, our first cousin, was to be married to Peter Drummond-Hay at the end of September, and all the wedding arrangements had been made when her father, Uncle Bob Davidson, became very ill. He had to have a transfusion and Peter came forward and gave his blood, but Uncle Bob died just before the wedding day. A subdued wedding took place, however, and Dad was there instead, to hold Clare's hand and give her away at Holy Trinity, Brompton. It was exactly two years previously that he had led Betty to her bridegroom in the little church at Bentley. But this time the bride was in black – ill-omened as it sadly proved to be.

By the end of October, Mum and Dad were all set to travel back to Kenya; Dad like a schoolboy eager to start on the journey home for the holidays. Rubbing his hands as he stood amongst the luggage, waiting for me to bring Jam-roll to the door, he said in his mock-American drawl, 'Well, Lady Powle, it's time we started for Africa,' and we drove through the London traffic to the South West India docks.

I dined with them on board and felt miserable; but luckily they didn't notice. Luckily they didn't realize, either, that this was the last time Dad was ever to leave England; it was an unofficial departure as they were coming back, so they said, sea-passages tentatively booked, for the spring-time of 1940.

The *Llandaff Castle* bore them away to Africa, and to Dad's last home, the little house at Nyeri. It stood close by the Outspan, with a view of the twin peaks of Mount Kenya rising above the clouds in vivid snow-whiteness. He had come back for the third and last time to this idyllic home which they named Pax-too, or Paxtu in 'complete' Swahili, to complete peace, with their own bit of garden laid out in front, centred round a shallow bird-bath. Here he could take his ease, painting and drawing, reading and writing and watching the antics of the birds giving themselves their daily baths. Hoopoes, fly-catchers, weaver-birds, all came and joined in his 'Bird Club', his favourites being the 'animated plums', small wren-like birds, well able to hold their own amongst their larger friends. It was not long before he had gathered enough material from this scene and from stories told to him about wild animals in the vicinity, to form a book called *Birds and Beasts in Africa* which he sent home for Mrs Wade to find a publisher. His pen was prolific, as was his paint-brush, but the difficulty now was to find a publisher prepared to take it on, as paper was in short supply and colour reproduction almost impossible. Some of his later paintings of animals were the best he had ever made, though sometimes he would lean back in his chair, saying 'I'm no artist'. 'Try with the other hand' we would tease him, knowing perfectly well that he was completely ambidexterous.

Mrs Wade not only found a publisher (Macmil-lan, later to be bombed out of their premises) but with all the yarns and sketches Dad sent back, was able to compile two more books, *Paddle your own Canoe* and *More Birds and Beasts*. It gave him infinite pleasure to be continuing to create something productive. My mother, kept sufficiently busy typing for him and trotting back and forth to the Post Office, was able to relax from her strenuous years of work to be at his side.

They had acquired a little hyrax, an affectionate small tree animal which would nestle in the crook of Mum's arm or sit on top of Dad's head, all furry and strokeable. It hid in the half-open drawer of his writing desk, would hop into the bottom one, scrabble up through the back and emerge through the top. Sometimes he was naughty and had to be scolded for nipping the shoots off the bouganvillea. 'Hyrie' he was called, and Mum had bought him as a baby for five pence, house-trained and living on a diet of rose petals. Dad had a box made for him to sleep in but I think Mum used to smuggle him into her bed as a hot-water bottle.

Left behind in England, I continued to be a deplorable secretary to Lady Kennet, helping to send out cards for Peter Scott's exhibition at Ackerman's and dealing with Lady Kennet's correspondence, mostly with Lord Francis Scott about the statue she had been commissioned to make of Lord Delamere, for the City of Nairobi.

Annie and Scofield kept Pax ticking over; Shawgm at last had had to be put to sleep; Dad had given Eccles, the caravan, to Gilwell on the borders of Epping Forest, and I delivered it there,

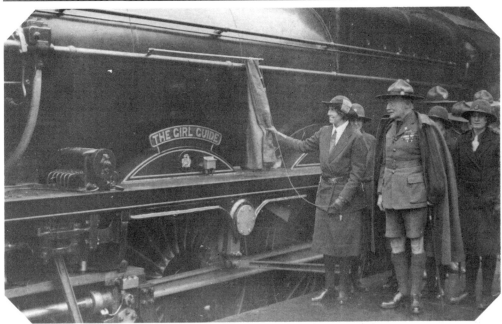

Naming 'The Girl Guide', 1930

Attending a levee with Colonel Sidney Kennedy, June 1937

*Above: Striking camp,
Gilwell Reunion, 1937 –
'Eccles' and 'Jam-roll'*

*Left: With Bill Hillcourt
– Boy Scouts of America,
World Jamboree, Holland,
1937*

*Right: Picnic preparations
at a Rally in Lithuania,
1930*

FUNCTIONS

Betty's wedding at Bentley, 24 September 1936

My sculpture of a polo player
(photographed by M.D. King)

King's Scout service, St George's Chapel, Windsor, 25 April 1937

At Nether Swell, with John [King], July 1938

AND FAMILY

before tucking Jam-roll up in the garage, against the day of their return; and of course I went to stay for several weekends with the Kings in their lovely Cotswold Stone house.

On completion of the Delamere statue, Lady Kennet was going off to Venice for a holiday in April and wouldn't need me for a month. Should I take this opportunity to dash out to Kenya? I wrote and asked my parents and by way of reply received a cheque from Dad to help with my air fare. If I could get there for Easter, they said, Betty would be there too, coming up from Northern Rhodesia and about to have her second baby. Mum was exultant in her delight at the prospect of having both daughters simultaneously approaching Nyeri from opposite directions. Cousin Christian David-son was already staying there, recuperating from a spine operation, and as well as being a splendid companion for my mother, was also taking her part as an 'odd-jobber' in the Outspan Hotel.

I went along to Charles Street and into the Imperial Airways office to book on the earliest flight. 'It will have to be on Good Friday,' they said. 'That's as good as any other Friday,' I replied. I wouldn't even have minded if it had been Friday the thirteenth! Dad had always consi-dered thirteen to be a lucky number in his family, 'and I wasn't in the 13th Hussars for nothing' he said.

I had a wondrous Easter flight to Lake Victoria; stepping into a flying boat at Southampton, it took four days to get there. We only flew in the day-time and had night halts at Rome, Alexan-dria, Khartoum and Kisumu. Clutched in my handbag I carried an important letter; it was from John, to give to my father, to ask if we could announce our engagement. Also I had a task detailed to me by Mrs Wade; I had to ask Dad, as tactfully as I could, where he wished to be buried, because Westminster Abbey had offered him a place!

Flying in to Nyeri, and greeting my parents, I shyly left John's envelope on the low, round table in Dad's sitting-room before going out with my mother to visit sister Betty in Dr Doig's nursing home. Betty had just achieved another family coincidence; she managed to give birth to Robin on 16th April, her own and her husband Gervas' joint birthday. What hope had I of being allowed to marry John? When he'd first asked me to marry him, I could only murmur, cautiously, 'When's your birthday?'

'November the fourth,' he replied, quizzically. 'No good, then,' said I, very sadly, because I would have liked to marry him, 'it's got to be on June 1st and the only people I've ever heard of with birthdays on June 1st are (Sir) Frank Whittle and (Sir) Andrew Horsbrugh-Porter, and I'm not in the running for either of them.'

'I'll change it then,' said John – but we had to wait till 1940 to achieve our hopes.

Next morning John's letter was still lying on the table exactly where I'd put it – unopened. Screw-ing up my courage I pushed it a bit nearer my father, saying in a voice that didn't sound like my own, 'There's a letter here for you, from John.'

'From John?' piped in my mother, 'Is that the young man with the long, low black car and the long, low black dog?'

At least they could picture him then. Tall and fair, with a black 'F' type Magna MG, and Tweenie, his shy mini black-and-tan dachshund, following close at his heels. 'Yes, that's him,' I cried, almost in despair, knowing our birthdays weren't right. Then, summoning my trump-card, I blurted out 'And he *did* play in goal for Charterhouse' – as Dad himself had done half a century or more before.

I'd done all I could. I'd played the ball into their court and now relaxed and made the most of my time with them, entering into and sharing this blissful life they were enjoying.

Alec Doig lent me his mare, Karoo (so-called because she was 'useless as a brood-mare, barren as the desert'), to ride every day, through the coffee shambas and banana plantations, fording the Chania River and back along the ridge by the golf-course or round through the native market in Nyeri. We played tennis, and Mum went off to her Swahili lessons. People were constantly calling in to sit on the verandah and chat, watching the antics of the wagtails and bul-buls at the bird-bath while Dumbhari, the head gardener, under his old slouch hat and with tinkling bells on his ears, pushed the mower over the springy green lawn.

Paxtu radiated happiness and sunshine. Migwe brought us early morning tea and we breakfasted together – in dressing-gowns as like as not – on the verandah; bowls of roses on the tables, sheafs of arum lilies in crocks by the verandah pillars. Even on dull days the garden seemed ablaze with flowers and the seasonal rain pattered down most evenings.

We motored out on some days, in the box-bodied Ford V.8., usually driven by Mahouri who was always ready to put on the chains if the mud was making the roads difficult. We went by a narrow grass track down to Dad's favourite fishing place on the Thega River and took picnics down to the bend where we could see four of the best trout pools.

The Stockleys, who lived ten miles out, at Mweiga, took us all out on to the Sangana Plain in our perpetual quest to see game. Through long grass and bushes, round hillsides and across streams, we saw great herds of Tommy gazelles, impala and oryx as well as zebra, eland, wart-hogs and jackal; ridiculous were those tall things, the secretary-birds and kavirondo cranes. We came back by Peases' farm, on to the road to Amboni, and home again quickly before a thunderstorm broke and heavy rain started lashing down.

Dad liked to 'do' the roses in their own bit of garden, also to help clear a way where the jacaranda was being cut back to give a better view. We walked down the well-stocked kitchen-garden into the valley with the Chania running below, Mum taking her trowel to dig up plants for Paxtu's flowerbeds. Vegetables were grown extensively here to supply the Outspan Hotel and all its personnel; cousin Christian came back here later on to manage this enterprise for the Walkers most efficiently. Artichokes grew in profusion, peas, figs, grapefruit, potatoes, coffee, tangerines, paw-paws, strawberrries – everything one could name, jumbled together, temperate or tropical – all would grow, and abundantly.

In the evenings we dined at the Outspan, or if Dad was not feeling strong enough he would stay in his room and one of us would dine with him. Eric and Bettie Walker often invited one or other of us to their own little house, adjacent to the Outspan, facing Nyeri Hill.

'Twiga,' Eric called to me one day, 'You're coming to have dinner with us tonight.' Twiga was Eric's name for me, being like a giraffe, tall, shy and ungainly, but with a sharp sense of the ridiculous. At dinner we met Captain Archie Ritch, the Chief Game Warden of Kenya, and his wife, and besides dining very well, we were fed on a wealth of animal stories, some frightening, others funny. Once I ventured to chip in, in my ignorance, 'What *is* the difference between a panther and a leopard?' Everybody looked at each other and I looked in the dictionary and had an assortment of replies. Dad had one of the quickest explanations: 'A panther,' he said, 'pants in the plains. A leopard leps in the low-lands and rocky hills, but they're both 'large, carniverous quadrupeds' according to that dictionary, and a leopard is a panther and a panther is a leopard. Does it just depend upon his habitat for which name he qualifies?

Talking of panthers (or leopards), perhaps the crowning enjoyment of all was another visit to 'Treetops', the 'house' Eric had had built – in true Peter Pan fashion – in a tree in the forest at the edge of the Aberdares. He had brought us all here on our first visit to Kenya three years previously and the enchantment of watching wild animals from a static position, at close range, was unbelievable then, even more so now, with improvements made for one's own creature comfort.

In the arms of a gigantic wild fig-tree two rooms had been built overlooking a large, oval-shaped clearing where wild animals were wont to come nightly to drink at the water's edge. Regular supplies of rock-salt were constantly laid out as a draw, to tempt them back. This was the Treetops that became famous overnight when King George VI died in 1952, for Princess Elizabeth and Prince Philip were staying there at the time, filming elephant. The Visitor's Book recorded that 'For the first time in the history of the world, a young Princess climbed up into a tree one day, and climbed down the next day, a Queen – God bless her.' Alas, during the Mau-mau rebellion, Treetops was burnt to the ground and what was left of its stump was soon destroyed by elephants rubbing themselves against it. Eric Walker, whilst the remains were still smouldering, stood with pencil and paper in hand, mapping out where a phoenix Treetops should arise. There was created the most sophisticated 'hide' the world has ever seen – Peter Pan's 'Wendy House' *in excelcis gloria*! The wonderful thing about it is that, despite all the comings and goings of Man building this house on tall, tree-trunk legs, the animals still come flocking to their drinking pool – just as before.

On our previous visit to the original Treetops we had seen, by the light of the full moon (nowadays they have reostatically controlled search-lights), any amount of wild animals, including elephant. They came so close under the tree that sister Betty and I, absolutely beside ourselves with excitement, felt compelled, in order to register contact with them, to spit on their backs. Eric thought it most unseemly, but it wasn't meant to be in any way derisive, and anyway the elephants didn't seem to mind.

This time we should exercise more decorum. This time, too, Dad, feeling his eighty-two years and a bit apprehensive of the walk uphill through the forest, asked Eric if he could ride the last bit of the trek, after we'd left the cars. Eric was filled with trepidation at the thought of the responsibility of leading the party along a narrow path with no room for a horse to turn and with the likelihood of a roaming rhino suddenly emerging from the bushes. Christian, with her bad back, said she didn't fancy the walk either; could she ride too? Eric demurred, but Dad insisted. 'It'll be all right,' he said airily. What could Eric do? He couldn't deny the request of a chap of eighty-two. So, 'Ugly' Sheldrick was called upon for assistance and he brought along a couple of horses, ready saddled. Eric slung his rifle over his shoulder and off we all went in single file up his well-worn jungle path and into the forest. All was well; it was mid-day and the wild animals had all made themselves invisible, there was silence in the forest – unless, gym-shoe clad, any one of us happened to step on a twig. Dad had conserved his strength to scale the 35-foot ladder up the tree; we all climbed up in turn and settled in quietly, awaiting nightfall. Except for meal-times we hardly moved, any of us, for the next twelve hours – Christian and I particularly, lying at full length on camp-beds on the balcony, chins cupped in hands, transfixed.

No animals came at first but we were entertained with a sort of overture by the anvil-birds clanging away, the bush cuckoos repeating their alternate note, one high, one low, and the hornbills, like ducks, quacking amongst themselves in the treetops. As dusk descended it was as though the stage was set and we watched intently to see which actor would be the first to appear and from which 'wing' of the amphitheatre it would approach.

Buck began to arrive as the light was fading, stepping delicately and moving towards the water's edge. It was a very short twilight; the moon rose quickly and soon we could see 'bushes' moving about, casting shadows as they went along in the moonlight. They were rhinos, being followed by forest hogs converging along the game trails leading to the pools, the pools in turn reflecting the light of the moon. Eric crept alongside us and whispered 'There's Belinda', indicating a massive rhino with a 'toto' bumping into its mother's side as they wallowed about, their feet making loud suction noises as they withdrew from the mud. The forest-pigs stood at a respectful distance, watching them.

Later on he swept the searchlight (powered by

car batteries) across the arena and picked up a black leopard stalking something in the grass. What was he stalking? A porcupine had appeared, backwards, with quills outspread, very angry. We watched two grumpy old rhinos squelching round one of the pools, looking for the salt, occasionally emitting crackling snorts, like a glorified horse's sneeze. By this time the 'orchestra' had struck up to no mean tune, led by the shrilling of the crickets, quite piercing at times and accompanied by low croakings from the bull-frogs. Other frogs, not the croaking ones, made a sort of watery whistle and there was a constant buzzing, like telegraph wires, from the bees.

Suddenly, to the right of the stage, an entire bush was hurled into the air, to be followed by a terrific crash. Slowly a rhino's face appeared – two great horns on his nose. He peered round, with a bit of bush still impaled on a horn, then withdrew again. Then he advanced, straight down one of the game trails, to the centre of the stage where some waterbuck were grazing. They were quickly on their feet and away, not great friends of rhino. He continued his rather dignified walk, paused for a sip from a nearby pool, then made an unhurried exit, giving his tummy a colossal slap with one stumpy hind-leg to beat off an insect.

Perpetual chattering came from high up in the branches where black and white colobus monkeys were gossiping, rather high-pitched and possibly concerned about a hyaena skulking about below, emitting a loud *hooo-aiou, hooo-aiou,* like a tug blowing its siren, and just as loud.

By 2 a.m. the moon had set and all was dark. We must have been dozing for some time, then woke in the pale morning light to see an almost constant parade of bush-buck, water-buck or dainty little duikers, their chestnut coats glossy in the early sunshine. By about 8 o'clock the performance was over and the actors had all dispersed off-stage for the day – Eric replenished us with food and mugs of coffee, then the safari porters arrived to accompany us all back 'down to earth' and home to Paxtu for a hot bath and a second large breakfast.

My holiday ended and I felt excessively cast down as I flew back to England, bearing my messages of NO to each request. Thank you for the honour, my father said, but No! he did not wish to be buried in Westminster Abbey, he'd rather his earthly remains be left to rest in Africa. And No, to John, we should not consider marriage until he'd qualified as a chartered accountant.

Sub-consciously, too, I may have known, although mercifully it didn't occur to me at the time, that I'd seen my father for the last time. My last sight of him was a lovely picture to hold in my mind. When I bent to kiss him good-bye he was sitting in his chair on the verandah of Paxtu, busily painting a picture of their garden, framed by tall gum trees and Mount Kenya, clad in eternal snows, beyond. I have this painting now; it's in the kitchen where I can look at it while I am waiting for the kettle to boil.

CHAPTER FOURTEEN

1939-41

The clouds of war rolled close again and broke, with that curious 'cold war' in September, 1939. Back in England, we'd all been trying to live through the summer as light-heartedly as we could. We went racing at Goodwood, a fortnight's camping in Cornwall, even getting passports ready to go driving about the Continent. There *couldn't* be a war! John, with his father and brother, was sailing about the south coast; always there were parties in London, friends' weddings with brides in white – and I was just having a smart new riding jacket made at 'Huntsman' the tailors in Saville Row.

I went into khaki uniform with many other girls for a week's A.T.S. camp at Mytchett, not far from Aldershot. We had fun driving ambulances and army lorries about, dodging in and out of pine trees, reversing up grassy slopes and slithering about in skid-pans and deep sand-tracks. We attended lectures on the 'infernal' combustion engine, were taught some stretcher drill and rudimentary first-aid and took our turn as mess orderlies in the cook-house, scrubbing down the trestle tables after meals.

Contact with my parents now relied entirely on postal communication and this became somewhat erratic; weeks went by without any letters, and then a bunch arrived together. Hearing on the radio the actual declaration of War, I found myself with some other A.T.S. staff car drivers at Hounslow hanging about outside Eastern Command Headquarters, awaiting orders to drive – we knew not where. Many hours were spent either sitting in our cars on the barrack square, studying our finger-nails, or, as the weather turned colder, huddled round an Aladdin heater in the old saddle-room of the Cavalry barracks, where the Greys used to keep their horses and where we now stabled our cars. Waiting, hopefully, to be summoned to drive a red-tabbed officer to the War Office in London.

Many a line I scrawled to my parents as I sat in 'my' Humber with its W.D. number painted on its side, foolscap or airmail paper propped on the steering wheel (or sometimes Eastern Command headed paper, pinched from the office of the M.G.A.). Often I thought, Oh! How merciful

Peter and Dad with Robert [the present Lord Baden-Powell]

Mum and Shawgm

At Pax Hill, with Twm

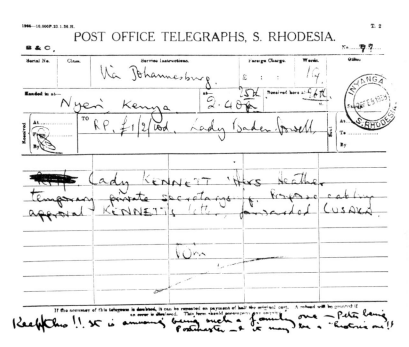

Me on Jority, my 21st Birthday present

FAMILY

Paxtu

John King

Paxtu
Nyeri
Kenya Colony.

19. Jan 39

My dear old Heather

Your letter just received saying you want your mind made up for you about coming out here at Easter – So Mum is toddling down to the telegraph office to send a cable saying "Come"

Volunteer B-P, No. W/1208 in staff car

Mum with Hyrie (above)

Reunion photograph, February 1940

WAR AND REUNION

that they were safely in Kenya, although even there they had the insecure feeling that the Italians might bulge out of Abyssinia and overflow into Kenya. Without my parents ever knowing it, a car, loaded with supplies and blankets, was kept permanently at the back of Paxtu, ready to transport them away southwards, should the awful occasion arise.

From Bentley Mrs Wade had to write and tell them what was happening at Pax, lying empty now, the staff all gone except for Annie and Scofield living at the lodge. Pax was to be commandeered by the War Department for the whole of the rest of the war and Twm, Dad's little Welsh terrier, became the beloved mascot, till his dying day, of the A.T.S. girls who were stationed there to run the canteen for the soldiers manning the ack-ack guns.

Mrs Wade contacted me, Volunteer B-P, No. W/1208, at Hounslow Barracks – 'You'd better come over and rescue what you want from Pax. Everything's going into store.'

So, all the Pax furniture was bundled away into vans and carted off to an unknown destination – a furniture repository. Not for the whole of the duration, however, for when poor Mum came sadly home – to no home – alone in 1942, her plight soon reached the ears of the Lord Chamberlain and she was immediately granted a 'Grace and Favour' apartment at Hampton Court. Out came the furniture again, blossoming into new surroundings.

In the grip of war now, John, having already been flying in the Civil Air Guard, was awaiting call-up into the R.A.F. and I was staff-car driver to a General. We put our heads together and wrote an imploring letter to my parents to ask if we could not now, with the pressure of war vitalizing our lives, announce our engagement? It took two months for a reply to come through, which firmly said we should wait until such time as John had 'received his Commission in His Majesty's Forces'. So, Volunteer W/1208, in her boiler suit, continued to clean the M.G.A.'s car – with a paraffin-soaked rag the camouflage paint could be made to shine beautifully! And John, still awaiting call-up, volunteered, with other amateur yachtsmen, for the Coastal Motor-boat Service, in the hope that this would bring forth some action.

The announcement of our engagement wouldn't exactly have hit the headlines when there were such dreadful things happening as the sinking of the *Royal Oak* in Scapa Flow and the *Rawalpindi* in deadly combat with the pocket battleship *Deutschland* off Iceland. Hitler had occupied Poland. Holland had flooded herself against invasion and Russia was annihilating Finland. The air was filled with suspense and waiting – waiting for something equally terrible to happen.

Sitting huddled over one knob of coal in the grate in my billet, I wrote to my parents at the end of October – two years after their Silver Wedding celebration – feeling most envious, but at the same time so thankful, they were warm and sitting in sunshine at Paxtu. The mail at this time was most precarious; some letters we received from each other safely, others never reached their destinations and many crossed in the post. A new invention, the 'airgraph', came into communications, but you couldn't divulge much on those.

A delighted letter came to me one day, however, from Mum to say that Peter and his family, and Betty with hers, had managed to get leave at the same time and all were travelling north to foregather at Nyeri simultaneously. It was about a fortnight before Dad's 83rd (and Mum's 51st) birthday and this proved to be his last family gathering, with Peter, Carine and little Robert; Gervas, Betty and their two, Gill and Robin. Many photographs were taken of this memorable occasion, mostly in the garden by Paxtu, with the little hyrax sitting on Mum's shoulder.

Dad's book, *Paddle your own Canoe* – with the alternative title he had put in the preface, 'Every tub must stand on its own bottom' – had just been published and although a copy was immediately sent to him, he never received it; it must have gone to the bottom of the sea. The first intimation he had of its publication was to see somebody else with it in their hands. On his last birthday, in February 1940, he wrote the foreword for his final book, *More Sketches in Kenya*, following on from *Birds and Beasts in Africa* which had come out the year previously. Sketches there were in plenty, full of humour, with rhinos dancing hand in hand, giraffes standing like cranes at work, birds squabbling at the bird-bath, and perhaps most enchanting of all, a line drawing, a wicked caricature of himself eating his breakfast while being watched by birds perched on the steps of the verandah at Paxtu.

Winter in England seemed endless, with snow thick upon the ground – 'Not deep, only another foot last night, Sir' – said the undaunted batman, sweeping the entrance steps to Headquarters, as the Staff officers arrived. Roads were appallingly slippery as well as bumpy from the packed snow and we drivers had orders to 'proceed' with all care. Despite trying to obey these instructions, I had no difficulty in driving my staff car, complete with General, straight into a snowdrift near Westgate, in the dark. Fortunately he found two army lorries to come to the rescue but by then I'd nearly shovelled a way out, woolly-gloved fingers tingling with cold, flapping great-coat cast aside.

In April, while parked by Pirbright parade-ground for the General to inspect a brigade of Guards, I penned a line to Kenya, remembering it was only this time last year that I had been staying with them for Easter. What a lot of water had flowed under the bridge since then. Now we were plunged deeper into the maelstrom of this war; Germany had overrun Denmark and although we had sunk *Bremen* and *Blücher*, the battle of Narvik had brought Norway into the conflict too.

Dad's voice was heard over the radio on St George's Day, broadcasting a message of courage throughout Britain, but unfortunately I missed hearing it. Hardly two weeks later, appealing to Great Britain for help, Belgium and Holland were invaded, soon to lay down their arms; Chamberlain resigned and Winston Churchill took up the reins. The Germans quickly overran Arras, Amiens and Abbeville, battle raged at Cambrai and before long came the evacuation of the B.E.F. from Dunkerque.

Groping with hooded headlamps, we were ordered to drive H.Q. staff by night to the south coast to see where troop trains had been requisitioned – ninety-one of them we'd seen rumbling by – bringing exhausted troops back from the Channel ports, some clad only in blankets tied round them with string. It was the end of the retreat from Dunkerque.

Paris was being bombed; Italy joined Germany and Winston Churchill gave out the news of the distaster of the withdrawal of the B.E.F. from France. The end of our world seemed near! On the day of the news that the Germans had entered Paris, I received this cable from Nyeri:

Airmail suspension delays correspondence otherwise had intended writing that owing to changed war conditions and directly John is right in His Majesty's Services we agree immediate announcement of engagement and marriage if you desire. Good luck dear and courage in facing war duties. All loving thoughts – BADEN-POWELL

Action Stations for John and me! He had received a call for interview at the Air Ministry and to attend a Medical Board and so in anticipation he'd set off to apply for a marriage licence.

I was sleeping in late one morning after being on night duty, when there came a call for me to go to the telephone in the sergeant's office. It was John.

'I've got it,' he said.

Pyjama-clad and tousled, and bare-footed in my haste to the office, I was a bit sleepy.

'What have you got?' I asked anxiously, thinking for an awful instant it might be measles.

'My Commission!'

Immediately we sent a telegram to my parents and, clutching the marriage licence, contacted the rector of Bentley, Canon le Fleming, to see if we could be married there the day after tomorrow. Everybody rallied round us. Mrs Wade and friends in Bentley filled the church with delphiniums and June flowers; the Thesigers, my guardians, took me to the church and afterwards held a champagne lunch party for us, and all John's family came over from Stow-on-the-Wold. I'd thrown off my uniform and climbed into a dress; Uncle B (Admiral) Thesiger, just home from bringing a convoy of fifty-four ships through from Gibraltar, led me to the altar – the same altar that Dad had escorted Betty to on her wedding in September, 1936. Church bells were no longer rung at weddings, being the signal that the Invasion had begun.

I think my parents were a bit taken aback to receive such a quick reaction to their cable. But they need never have worried, nor need they have had any qualms when Betty was married, since we have all, Peter too, passed our 25-year 'milestones' and celebrated Silver Weddings, just as they had done themselves. Within six months of our wedding, however, Dad had died.

Mum reported in her letters in August that often he was running a temperature – it went up and down, 'More up than down', and that he was feeling 'more down than up'. No ointment was giving relief to the itching he suffered on his hands and legs. She had taken him to Nairobi in September for radium treatment but that had had no good results either. The specialist again pronounced a very tired heart. Although he tried to keep on sketching and drawing, and in October managed to design a Christmas card, he had little energy left and little wish to live.

Cousin Christian came back to Nyeri after helping Betty with her family at Chinsali for six months and was a tower of strength to Mum, who knew within herself, but found it hard to face up to the fact that his life was ebbing away. On Christmas Day, 1940, he summoned up enough strength to sit up in his chair and listen to the King's speech, broadcast throughout the world. He lived through into the New Year, although hardly conscious now, and quietly slipped away in the early hours of 8th January, 1941 – within six weeks of his eighty-fourth birthday.

I felt helpless, cooped up here in war-stricken England, for besides my own personal grief I felt so worried for poor Mum. It was merciful that Christian was there to hold her hand and lead her away, motoring to Rhodesia; Eric Walker, Dad's age-long friend, was away up on the northern frontier with the 1st South African Division,

'facing the Italian hordes advancing on Kenya'. When he received the bad news he immediately took leave, but by the time he'd journeyed 400 miles across the desert, he reached Nyeri only in time to join in the military cortège as it went on its sad way to the cemetery.

By this time one could but feel that Dad, himself, his spirit released from all earthly suffering, was glad the time had come to be taken to his last resting-place. He had prepared himself, leaving messages to be read 'in the event of my death'. 'Be Prepared' had been the motto by which he lived and disciplined himself and which he handed on to the Movements he had founded, and thus he was prepared to die.

I keep, in the fly-leaf of my Bible, a scruffy little bit of paper on which he'd pencilled:

That when I pass away I may say that at any rate I did my best.

Being mortals, we know we all must die, some achieving fame on their way, others slipping away, hardly making a mark. We can but presume that God keeps a register of us all, having had some reason for the existence of each one of us. I like to think that I shall see my parents together again, in eternal bliss, a hyrax on my mother's shoulder.

As a tail-piece, I would flash back many years, to when I was a very new schoolgirl, sitting shyly at my desk, legs entwined round the chair, my

neighbour, Ann Killick, looked across at me once or twice, paused in her pen-knifing of yet another horse's head on her form-room desk and said 'What do they mean by saying your father's the *founder* of the Scouts – there've *always* been Scouts!'